BCBA
Mock Exam

185 Questions & Answers with Explanations.
Test your knowledge in Applied Behavior Analysis.
5th Edition Task List

Brain LAB

TABLE OF CONTENTS

The Future BCBA is Studying

BCBA Mock Exam :
185 Questions & Answerwith Explanations.
Test your knowledge in Applied Behavior Analysis.
5th Edition Task List

Shhhh...

QUESTIONS

1) A BCBA is providing services to a client who is receiving services from another behavior analyst. The BCBA becomes aware that the other behavior analyst is violating the ethical code. According to the ethical code, what should the BCBA do in this situation?

   A. Continue providing services to the client and ignore the other behavior analyst's ethical violations

   B. Report the other behavior analyst's ethical violations to the appropriate authorities

   C. Confront the other behavior analyst about their ethical violations and attempt to resolve the issue informally

   D. Consult with other professionals before making a decision about how to proceed

2) A lot of kids in your classroom talk too loudly at lunch. Which contingency would be best to use?

   A. If the noise level stays below a specific level, the entire class gets an additional five minutes of break.

   B. The entire class receives an additional five minutes of recess if the loudest student maintains a noise level below a certain level.

   C. Each student who keeps his voice low gets 5 extra minutes of recess.

   D. The teacher selects students she sees talking quietly and awards them 5 extra minutes of recess.

3) You work with a child who has autism, you give her a toy if she claps her hands and a strawberry if she taps her nose. You're using a:

   A. Multiple schedule reinforcer assessment.

   B. Multiple stimulus preference assessment.

   C. Concurrent schedule reinforcer assessment.

   D. Progressive ratio schedule reinforcer assessment.

4) A BCBA is working with a client who has limited verbal communication skills. The client's parent requests that the BCBA use a communication device that has not been scientifically validated as a behavior intervention. According to the ethical code, what should the BCBA do in this situation?

   A. Agree to the parent's request and use the communication device as a behavior intervention

   B. Refuse the parent's request and explain why the use of a non-scientifically validated communication device is not an appropriate behavior intervention

   C. Use the communication device as a behavior intervention but only if it is the client's preferred method of intervention

   D. Consult with other professionals before making a decision about using a non-scientifically validated communication device as a behavior intervention

5) What is the Skinner box?

   A. A device used in operant conditioning experiments

   B. A tool used to measure respondent behavior

   C. A technique used in classical conditioning

   D. A type of punishment procedure

6) A BCBA is conducting a functional analysis on a child with a history of aggressive behavior. During the alone condition, the child engages in self-injurious behavior (SIB) for a total of 3 minutes over the 10-minute session. During the attention condition, the child engages in SIB for a total of 6 minutes over the 10-minute session. During the play condition, the child engages in SIB for a total of 1 minute over the 10-minute session. What can be concluded from these data?

   A. The alone condition may have served as an establishing operation for the attention and play conditions.

   B. The attention condition may have functioned as a maintaining variable for the child's SIB.

   C. The play condition may have functioned as an abolishing operation for the child's SIB.

   D. (All of the above).

7) Radical behaviorism states that:

   A. Private events are unobservable and should be excluded from the analysis of behavior.

   B. The study of behavior should consist of direct observation of environmental events and events within the organism should be ignored.

   C. Private events are the same as the public events other than the fact that they are unobservable by others.

   D. States of mind and mental processes are the proper subject matter of psychology.

8) Luca requests a toy car from his father and he gives it to him. Luca continues to ask for the toy car. This is:

   A. Negative reinforcement.

   B. Positive reinforcement.

   C. Respondent behavior.

   D. Automatic positive reinforcement.

9) ABA (Applied behavior analysis):

   A. Creates the basis for the development of EAB (experimental analysis of behavior).

   B. Is antithetical to the experimental analysis of behavior.

   C. Frequently takes results from the EAB to problems in the lab.

   D. Frequently takes the results of the EAB and applies them to social problems.

10)   A BCBA is evaluating the effectiveness of a token economy intervention for a child with ADHD. The BCBA collects data on the number of on-task behaviors during baseline and intervention sessions. Which graph should the BCBA use to display the data?

   A. Bar graph

   B. Line graph

   C. Pie chart

   D. Scatterplot

11)   James, a BCBA, is asked by his boss to work with a new client with Pica disorder. James does not have prior experience working in that area and he only attended a panel discussion about Pica at an accredited conference. What's the best thing to do for James?

   A. James should collaborate with another BCBA familiar with pica disorder and ask for their recommended practices.

   B. James should explore scientific publications and incorporate their insights, in addition to the conference's content.

   C. Apart from the panel, the BCBA should consider consulting with experts in pica and eating disorders.

   D. Simply attending a panel discussion about pica doesn't automatically qualify one to treat eating disorder problems.

12)   A reflex is a:

   A. Conditioned stimulus and its related ontogenic history.

   B. Response and its related ontogenic history.

   C. Conditioned stimulus and its related controlling stimulus.

   D. Response and its related controlling stimulus.

13)   What does not describe EAB (Experimental Analysis of Behavior)?

   A. Behaviorism serves as its foundation.

   B. It is a technique for researching behavior in natural environments.

   C. It requires ongoing observation or measurement.

   D. It serves as the starting point for many solutions to significant societal issues.

14)   What best illustrates a stimulus-stimulus relation?

   A. Smartphone and a screen tap, as one evokes the other.

   B. Screen tap and an app opening, because one is contingent on the other.

   C. Smartphone and a tablet, because both evoke screen tapping behavior.

   D. (All of the above)

15)   An intervention is supported by peer-reviewed experimentation, but you don't think it will work because the results are inconsistent with what operant conditioning would predict:

A. Accept the data because it reflects a new approach.

B. Reject this research on the grounds that it contradicts Skinner's writings.

C. Reject this research because operant conditioning is a well-established fact.

D. Accept the data that supports the intervention unless different findings are found.

16)   An exploitative relationship could be with:

A. Coworkers within your agency.

B. The general public.

C. Other professionals serving the same client.

D. Students or research participants.

17)   In a FA (functional analysis), the "Play Condition" is also called the "Control condition" for the others because:

A. A caregiver continually provides attention throughout the session.

B. Preferred items and activities are easily available during the session or provided on a continuous or dense schedule of reinforcement.

C. Throughout the session, no demands are presented.

D. (All of the above)

18)   During sessions with your client Paul, you noticed that praise, tokens (exchangeable for snacks), and candies are equally effective as reinforcers. You should use:

A. A rotation that includes all three.

B. Praise.

C. Tokens.

D. Candies.

19)   A new student, who was just transferred from a different school, starts stealing things off the teacher's desk. The BCBA looks at the student's FBA from eight months ago. The FBA states that 'Escape' is the function of this behavior. Should the BCBA develop an intervention using these results?

A. Yes, as long as the FBA is signed by a BCBA.

B. No, the BCBA should only use FBA data he collected himself.

C. No, a new FBA should be conducted.

D. Yes, because the same behavior has re-emerged within one year.

20)   Two brothers are screaming in their room, when their father reprimands them and they stop (and remain quiet). For the kids, the reprimand serves as:

    A. Positive reinforcement.

    B. Extinction.

    C. Punishment.

    D. Negative reinforcement.

21)   A child who exhibits unpredictable tantrums. Which of the following reflects a deterministic philosophy:

    A. "We haven't yet identified the factors that control tantrums."

    B. "Tantrums are the result of a personality disorder."

    C. "The behavior is consistent with the DSM diagnosis of intermittent explosive disorder."

    D. "Our data support that tantrums are a function of depressive moods."

22)   During an FA escape condition, the discriminative stimulus is provided by:

    A. The individual engaged in an activity in a room by him or herself.

    B. A therapist doing a preferred activity with the child.

    C. A therapist in the same room with the individual, but engaging in other activities such as reading a magazine.

    D. The therapist prompting the child to engage in various tasks, for example, gross motor exercises.

23)   Which is an unconditioned stimulus?

    A. The smell of food

    B. The touch of your finger on a hot surface

    C. The cold breeze on your skin

    D. (All of the above)

24)   Which stimuli may belong to the same stimulus class?

    A. A picture of a carrot, a carrot, a bunny

    B. A whistle at a sports game and a raised red flag

    C. A chocolate bar, a candy, hearing "No!"

    D. (All of the above)

25)   A BCBA is conducting a preference assessment with a child who has autism spectrum disorder. The BCBA presents the child with two toys and measures the duration of engagement with each toy. The results show that the child engages with Toy A for an average of 2 minutes and Toy B for an average of 1 minute. What type of preference assessment was conducted?

   A. Forced-choice assessment

   B. Single-item assessment

   C. Paired-stimulus assessment

   D. Multiple-stimulus without replacement assessment

26)   Following the Ethic Code that guides their profession, Behavior Analysts do not have sexual or romantic relationships with parents, clients, or supervisees:

   A. Within 4 years of the end of the professional relationship.

   B. Ever, even after the end of the professional relationship.

   C. Within 2 years of the end of the professional relationship.

   D. Within 6 months of the end of the professional relationship.

27)   James is taught that Cane means Dog and that Dog means Perro. Which is a derived relation?

   A. James knows that Cane means Perro.

   B. James knows that Cane is a Dog.

   C. James knows that Dog is Perro.

   D. (All of the above)

28)   Every time you hit the power button on your television remote, the TV turns on. What kind of reinforcement schedule is this indicative of?

   A. FR0

   B. CRF (or FR1)

   C. F11

   D. VR1

29)   Tom is a salesperson calling potential clients. On what kind of reinforcement schedule will he likely receive positive responses?

   A. A compound schedule of reinforcement

   B. An FR schedule of reinforcement

   C. A VI schedule of reinforcement

   D. A VR schedule of reinforcement

30)   A BCBA and a client's family have verbally agreed upon a treatment plan, including the specific duties, the weekly session time, and the payment terms. What is a critique to this approach?

A. This is a great example of a well-defined, professional role because the critical issues have been agreed upon.

B. Verbal agreements are sufficient.

C. Although these key issues have been shared, they should have been communicated in writing and signed from both parties.

D. The BCBA should not have specified the amount of time per week, because it varies from child to child.

31)   Jenny wants to increase her studying behavior. For every 10 pages she reads, she will give herself about 5 minutes of break time. Which schedules of reinforcement is Jenny using?

A. Fixed interval (FI) and variable interval (VI)

B. Fixed ratio (FR) and variable ratio (VR)

C. Fixed ratio (FR) and variable interval (VI)

D. Fixed interval (FI) and variable ratio (VR)

32)   A comprehensive behavioral assessment should determine:

A. Competing contingencies.

B. Generalization and maintenance factors.

C. Possible punishers and/or reinforcers.

D. (All of the above)

33)   Spontaneous recovery is:

A. Short lived a followed by an increase in behavior

B. The re-emergence of behavior during extinction

C. A warning that the extinction is ineffective

D. (All of the above)

34)   The data collected over the past month in the English class, indicate that whenever the teacher walks in the class, on-task behavior increases:

A. This demonstrates a functional relationship.

B. Extinction is demonstrated.

C. This demonstrates a causal relationship.

D. Punishment is demonstrated.

35)   A parent confesses holding his child down during tantrums to protect him from severe SIB that would cause injuries. This has resulted in a few minor bruises, but the child does not seem distressed. The BCBA:

A. Reports the family to the appropriate protective services agency.

B. Documents the parent's confession, but no further action is needed.

C. Advises the parent to receive training in crisis management and restraint.

D. Does nothing since the parent does not appear to be hurting the child.

36)   A worker on an assembly line is compensated for completing a package of 12 assemblies. Per package, he earns $1 for assembly A and $1.50 for assembly B. Each assembly requires roughly the same amount of time and effort. If the employee is permitted to choose, he will likely solely work on assembly B. Based on what behavioral principle can you derive this?

A. Behavioral contrast

B. Behavioral momentum

C. Matching law

D. (None of the above)

37)   When practicing with flashcards, a child often escapes the work area when asked to read a difficult word. What would be the best solution to solve this?

A. The matching law by increasing the number of tokens earned for reading difficult words and reducing the tokens earned for math facts.

B. Behavioral momentum by scheduling preferred activities (recess and math) before reading.

C. Behavioral contrast by allowing escape from difficult tasks at other times.

D. Using high-p sequence by having 3 easy words precede each hard word.

38)   A client who has previously harmed others has threatened to harm another individual. You:

A. May be legally responsible to report this, but only if the client consents.

B. May be responsible for preventing the client from hurting others, but you cannot disclose confidential information.

C. May be legally responsible to report this to the police.

D. Ethically cannot report it to anyone except his legal guardian (if he has one).

39)   Before requesting a supervisee to perform a new assignment, the supervising BCBA should assess:

A. How many times the supervisee has previously attempted and completed that task, respectively.

B. If the supervisee has the skills to perform that task competently, ethically, and safely.

C. If the supervisee is interested in performing that task.

D. If there is a need for the skills in this setting and for this population.

40)   To improve ecological validity in a FA (functional analysis) you could:

A. Incorporate the client's familiar people (parents, caregivers or peers) from the natural setting into the FA.

B. Conduct the FA in the natural setting (for example, the client's home).

C. Include in the experimental setting furniture, décor and toys from the natural setting.

D. (All of the above)

41)   Mike is teaching his fish, Finny, to swim to the top of the tank when he taps on the glass by feeding it after each tap. Over time, Finny swims to the top every time Mike taps, even when there's no food. What form of conditioning has taken place with Finny's learned behavior?

A. Operant conditioning

B. Respondent conditioning

C. Observational learning

D. None of the above

42)   John, a college professor, notices his students are using their smartphones too much during class, so he establishes a rule limiting smartphone use. However, he finds that the students' rate of passing notes during class increases dramatically. This scenario illustrates:

A. Contingency shaped behavior.

B. Behavioral contrast.

C. Behavioral momentum.

D. Matching law.

43)   A basketball player realizes that when the coach claps his hands in a certain way, it's a signal for a more aggressive defensive strategy. He has learned to take advantage of these moments to request substitutions as the coach is more likely to accept. This scenario illustrates:

A. Stimulus discrimination.

B. Response generalization.

C. Response maintenance.

D. Stimulus generalization.

44)   A child is receiving candies during the session. Instead of attending to the instructional stimuli, he stares at the candy, attempts to open the jar, argues with the BCBA for permission to hold the container on his knee, etc. He is not focusing enough, and he is unable to complete the tasks so he doesn't earn any candy. The instructor should:

A. Work more on compliance goals or change to simpler tasks so that the child can start earning reinforcers.

B. Do not use M&Ms as reinforcers.

C. Use a less strong reinforcer or use tokens to exchange for candies at the end.

D. (All of the above)

45) A worker has been trained to inspect bottles of beer as they pass a light on a conveyor belt and to remove any bottles containing darker wine. Later, the same task is given to him at a different station on the assembly line. His successful completion of the same assignment in the new location is a demonstration of:

A. Response generalization.

B. Stimulus generalization.

C. Concept generalization.

D. (All of the above)

46) Self-injury may sometimes function to:

A. Produce sensory stimulation.

B. Access tangible items.

C. Access a TV show.

D. (All of the above)

47) Which of the following exemplifies response generalization?

A. After being taught to tie his shoelaces using a training shoe, a child is able to tie his shoelaces on his own shoes.

B. A student, who has learned to solve addition problems during the school year, can still solve these problems after coming back from winter vacation.

C. A girl learns to play a song on the piano using her right hand, and later, she is also able to play it using her left hand.

D. (All of the above)

48) Lisa says, "I want video games." Her friend reacts by suggesting, "We should probably play something fun." What does this type of response from Lisa's friend demonstrate?

A. An echoic.

B. A mand.

C. An intraverbal.

D. A tact.

49) Two behavior analysts are conducting IOA on a data collection procedure. The first observer records a target behavior as occurring, while the second observer records it as not occurring. What should the behavior analysts do?

A. Disregard the IOA results and continue with data collection

B. Discuss the discrepancy and work together to improve their agreement

C. End the data collection procedure and start over

D. Write in the soap notes that the IOA is 50%

50)   What are the antecedent stimulus and the consequence in the final step of a tact transfer procedure? Fill in as: Antecedent stimulus is _____, and the consequence is _____.

A. Nonverbal stimulus, generalized conditioned reinforcement

B. MO, the given item

C. Verbal stimulus to respond, generalized conditioned reinforcement

D. Nonverbal stimulus, the given item

51)   A child's stomach growls, and he asks for a cookie. The cookie jar and his parent are present. This is a:

A. Mand under the control of an MO (deprivation of food) and an SD (sight of the cookie jar).

B. Mand under the control of sight of cookie jar and parent present (SD).

C. Mand under the control of deprivation of food (MO).

D. MO under the control of a mand.

52)   Suppose you wanted to understand how to change gears in a manual car. After going through a driving course and following the steps of the procedure, you are now able to change gears smoothly. The act of changing gears is now an example of what?

A. Verbally reinforced behavior.

B. Rule-governed behavior.

C. Direct acting contingencies.

D. Contingency-shaped behavior.

53)   During an experiment called "delayed gratification" at a pizzeria, 10 customers were each presented with a small slice of pizza and informed, "If you don't eat this slice for 7 minutes, you'll receive 7 larger slices." The decision of the customers who waited exemplifies:

A. Contingency-shaped behavior.

B. Cognitive dissonance.

C. Rule-governed behavior.

D. Behavior reinforced by direct-acting contingencies.

54)   Which of the following behaviors most likely indicates a function?

A. Falling during walks often results in a bruise.

B. Masturbation results in others pretending it doesn't happen.

C. Hitting others always results in remorse.

D. Scratching results in relief from itching.

55)   A Behavior Analyst provides services to a client, and also has a personal relationship with the client's parent. According to the ethical code, what should the BCBA do in this situation?

A. Continue providing services to the client and maintain the personal relationship with the parent

B. End the personal relationship with the parent and continue providing services to the client

C. End the professional relationship with the client and the personal relationship with the parent

D. End the personal relationship with the parent and refer the client to another behavior analyst

56)   Sarah is hungry and you are teaching her to say "Fork." You give her a plate of food but without a fork. With respect to saying "Fork," the food with no fork function as:

A. A UMO.

B. A CMO-T.

C. A CMO-S.

D. An SD.

57)   You are driving in the Arizona desert low on gas. You see a lighted gas station sign in the distance and take the next exit. The gas station is:

A. An SD.

B. A CMO-T

C. A conditioned reinforcer.

D. An MO.

58)   You start reading a book, but the text seems blurry. The unclear words might have an:

A. Evocative effect on looking for the reading glasses.

B. Abative effect on reading.

C. Abative effect on requesting additional reading material.

D. (All of the above)

59)   When the Occupational Therapist walks into the room, the student with whom he will be working starts to throw a tantrum. This delays the therapy session from starting right away. The OT arrival:

A. Is a CMO-T.

B. Is a conditioned punisher.

C. Is a CMO-S.

D. Is a CMO-R.

60) Guiding a shopper to select a particular product by strategically placing it closer to more easily accessible to the shopper than its competitors is primarily known as a:

A. Movement cue.

B. Physical cue.

C. Position cue.

D. Redundancy cue.

61) A BCBA is working with a child who engages in SIB (self-injurious behavior). The behavior analyst conducts an FA (functional analysis) and determines that the behavior is maintained by escape from academic demands. What type of intervention is most appropriate in this scenario?

A. Differential reinforcement of other behavior (DRO)

B. Noncontingent reinforcement (NCR)

C. Functional communication training (FCT)

D. Response blocking

62) A new behavior analyst is having difficulty understanding how to complete an assessment. What type of supervision would be most appropriate in this scenario?

A. Group supervision

B. Individual supervision

C. Peer supervision

D. Self-supervision

63) Rating scales used for functional assessment are a type of?

A. Direct method.

B. Analog assessment.

C. Functional analysis.

D. Indirect method.

64) Emily was in a car accident and was injured. Whenever she hears a car horn, she becomes anxious and fearful. Which type of conditioning is involved in Emily's reaction to hearing a car horn?

A. Operant conditioning

B. Respondent conditioning

C. Observational learning

D. None of the above

65)   After touching a hot stove, your hand feels a sharp pain. This pain:

A. Evokes behaviors that soothe the burn and might abate touching hot surfaces again (punitive effect).

B. Acts as an SD for behavior that alleviate the burn and abates touching hot surfaces.

C. Abates the current behavior and may act as an AO (abolishing operation) for future behaviors that might result in soothing the burn.

D. Evokes the current behavior and may act as an EO (establishing operation) for future behaviors that might result in soothing the burn.

66)   The martial arts instructor wanted to decrease the number of trials it took his student to perform a technique correctly. Which measure would be the most useful?

A. Celeration

B. Trials to criterion

C. Duration

D. Frequency

67)   Stimulus generalization could be described in everyday language as:

A. "The occurrence of new behavior from skills the person previously learned."

B. "The occurrence of a behavior in the presence of a different stimulus than the one used in training."

C. "Being able to apply something learned in class in a different setting."

D. "The occurrence of a trained behavior in a novel or untrained setting."

68)   A behavior analyst is supervising a trainee who is consistently arriving late for supervision meetings. What should the behavior analyst do?

A. Ignore the trainee's tardiness

B. Address the issue with the trainee and discuss the importance of punctuality

C. Cancel supervision meetings with the trainee

D. Call the BCBA to communicate his nonprofessional behavior

69)   Which of the following behaviors should Event recording not be used to measure?

A. Mands

B. Words read

C. Crying

D. (All of the above)

target behavior is dangerous, baseline:

 be conducted by staff members trained in restraint procedures.

 be conducted by large staff members.

 conducted but should be brief.

ot be possible due to safety concerns.

h of the following could be a DV (dependent variable) for a child in a classroom?

sion

 which the teacher delivers reinforcement

er of correct math problems completed in a minute

from onset to completion

ing collaboratively with another professional or paraprofessional means:

ing blood levels and psychotropic medications on the same graph to analyze blood levels and shar-
ith the psychiatrist.

cting a preference assessment to identify potential reinforcers that staff will use in your program.

ing target behaviors and the current medications on the same graph to evaluate psychotropic medi-
fect and share this with the psychiatrist.

 the above)

avior analyst is supervising a BCaBA who is conducting a functional assessment. What should the
lyst do to ensure the assessment is being conducted ethically?

ve the BCaBA's sessions and provide feedback

 the BCaBA with written instructions and checklists

 in with the BCaBA periodically but allow them to work independently

he BCaBA record the assessment sessions for review later

lternating treatments design controls for:

nce effects.

alization effects.

mentation issues.

ncy effects.

70) The practitioner noted an improvement in the client's rate of completing the laundry task's steps per 10 minutes of session that was X2 (times 2) different from the two response rates. What kind of measurements did the BCBA take?

A. Duration

B. Rate

C. Celeration

D. Trials to criterion

71) "The test scores are consistently high. However, we doubt the _____ of the test due to the possibility of someone else taking it and adding their name on it."

A. Reliability.

B. Accuracy.

C. Validity.

D. Interobserver Agreement.

72) Assessment results must:

A. Not be shared with the client unless there is a clinical need to do so.

B. Be explained in an easy and understandable language to the client and client's surrogate.

C. Be explained to the client's surrogate; they do not need to be explained to the client.

D. Be displayed consistent with practices in the field and described in technical language.

73) A company wants to increase sales of a particular product. The behavior analyst recommends providing a discount to customers who purchase multiple units of the product. What type of reinforcement schedule is being used in this scenario?

A. Variable interval - VI

B. Fixed interval - FI

C. Variable ratio - VR

D. Fixed ratio - FR

74) What are 3 different assessment procedures to determine the function of a target behavior?

A. Direct assessments, topographical assessments, and FA (functional analyses).

B. Direct assessments, indirect assessments, and functional analyses.

C. Functional assessments, topographical assessments, and checklists.

D. Indirect assessments, direct assessments, and functional assessments.

75)   A child with autism has difficulty communicating their needs and wants. The behavior analyst recommends using a picture exchange communication system (PECS) to teach the child to request items. What is the primary function of PECS in this scenario?

   A. To establish a new behavior

   B. To reduce problem behavior

   C. To increase social skills

   D. To decrease anxiety

76)   The disparity between his high initial score and the much lower result in the retest brings the focus on the test's _____.

   A. Accuracy.

   B. Reliability.

   C. Validity.

   D. Difficulty.

77)   A researcher attempts to gather data from a position where the students will be unaware of his presence due to:

   A. Observer drift.

   B. Reactivity.

   C. Expectancy.

   D. Complexity.

78)   A BCBA has a client who is not making progress with the current behavior intervention plan. The BCBA is unsure of the next steps to take to modify the behavior intervention plan. According to the ethical code, what should the BCBA do in this situation?

   A. Continue with the current behavior intervention plan and wait for the client to make progress

   B. Consult with other professionals to determine the appropriate next steps

   C. Discontinue services with the client

   D. Modify the behavior intervention plan without consulting with anyone else

79)   A supervisee claims that her supervisor is severe, frequently ignores her accomplishments, and is extremely critical of her, even for little mistakes. This is an ethical issue because:

   A. BCBA supervisors are required to provide performance-enhancing feedback to supervisees.

   B. It involves use of aversive procedures without reinforcement.

   C. The Code indicates that the BACB is to be notified if supervisors don't provide feedback in a way that benefits the supervisee.

   D. It is a personal conflict.

80)   A practitioner compared the math fact performance measurements of a new _____ generated by a computer program for math facts. This is a method for evaluating:

   A. Validity of the data.

   B. Reliability of the data.

   C. Accuracy of the data.

   D. IOA.

81) During an observation session, a practitioner compared the SIB measureme _____ another observer. This is a method for evaluating:

   A. Reliability of the data collection procedure.

   B. Believability of the data.

   C. Interobserver agreement.

   D. Validity

82)   Reviewing records:

   A. Could give you information on previously effective treatments, which sh _____

   B. May yield information on the function(s) of the problem behavior(s), alt _____ change more than they stay the same.

   C. Are likely to give information about how well past treatments worked (e _____ about how well observers agreed with each other (IOA) and how well the _____ rity).

   D. Could yield identification of a past treatment that has been ineffective a _____

83)   Which of the following is a factor that can affect the validity of a func _____

   A. The use of a single setting for the analysis

   B. The use of multiple participants for the analysis

   C. The use of a latency-based measurement system

   D. The use of a restricted range of antecedent stimuli

84)   Over time, the IOA between two observers gets better because they _____ standing about how to score topographies of the behavior, which is differe _____ This is known as:

   A. Expectancy.

   B. Observer drift.

   C. Reactivity.

   D. B and C.

70) The practitioner noted an improvement in the client's rate of completing the laundry task's steps per 10 minutes of session that was X2 (times 2) different from the two response rates. What kind of measurements did the BCBA take?

A. Duration

B. Rate

C. Celeration

D. Trials to criterion

71) "The test scores are consistently high. However, we doubt the _____ of the test due to the possibility of someone else taking it and adding their name on it."

A. Reliability.

B. Accuracy.

C. Validity.

D. Interobserver Agreement.

72) Assessment results must:

A. Not be shared with the client unless there is a clinical need to do so.

B. Be explained in an easy and understandable language to the client and client's surrogate.

C. Be explained to the client's surrogate; they do not need to be explained to the client.

D. Be displayed consistent with practices in the field and described in technical language.

73) A company wants to increase sales of a particular product. The behavior analyst recommends providing a discount to customers who purchase multiple units of the product. What type of reinforcement schedule is being used in this scenario?

A. Variable interval - VI

B. Fixed interval - FI

C. Variable ratio - VR

D. Fixed ratio - FR

74) What are 3 different assessment procedures to determine the function of a target behavior?

A. Direct assessments, topographical assessments, and FA (functional analyses).

B. Direct assessments, indirect assessments, and functional analyses.

C. Functional assessments, topographical assessments, and checklists.

D. Indirect assessments, direct assessments, and functional assessments.

75) A child with autism has difficulty communicating their needs and wants. The behavior analyst recommends using a picture exchange communication system (PECS) to teach the child to request items. What is the primary function of PECS in this scenario?

A. To establish a new behavior

B. To reduce problem behavior

C. To increase social skills

D. To decrease anxiety

76) The disparity between his high initial score and the much lower result in the retest brings the focus on the test's _____.

A. Accuracy.

B. Reliability.

C. Validity.

D. Difficulty.

77) A researcher attempts to gather data from a position where the students will be unaware of his presence due to:

A. Observer drift.

B. Reactivity.

C. Expectancy.

D. Complexity.

78) A BCBA has a client who is not making progress with the current behavior intervention plan. The BCBA is unsure of the next steps to take to modify the behavior intervention plan. According to the ethical code, what should the BCBA do in this situation?

A. Continue with the current behavior intervention plan and wait for the client to make progress

B. Consult with other professionals to determine the appropriate next steps

C. Discontinue services with the client

D. Modify the behavior intervention plan without consulting with anyone else

79) A supervisee claims that her supervisor is severe, frequently ignores her accomplishments, and is extremely critical of her, even for little mistakes. This is an ethical issue because:

A. BCBA supervisors are required to provide performance-enhancing feedback to supervisees.

B. It involves use of aversive procedures without reinforcement.

C. The Code indicates that the BACB is to be notified if supervisors don't provide feedback in a way that benefits the supervisee.

D. It is a personal conflict.

80)   A practitioner compared the math fact performance measurements of a newly trained observer to a report generated by a computer program for math facts. This is a method for evaluating:

A. Validity of the data.

B. Reliability of the data.

C. Accuracy of the data.

D. IOA.

81) During an observation session, a practitioner compared the SIB measurements of one observer to those of another observer. This is a method for evaluating:

A. Reliability of the data collection procedure.

B. Believability of the data.

C. Interobserver agreement.

D. Validity

82)   Reviewing records:

A. Could give you information on previously effective treatments, which should be avoided.

B. May yield information on the function(s) of the problem behavior(s), although functions frequently change more than they stay the same.

C. Are likely to give information about how well past treatments worked (efficacy), as well as information about how well observers agreed with each other (IOA) and how well the process worked (procedural integrity).

D. Could yield identification of a past treatment that has been ineffective and should be avoided.

83)   Which of the following is a factor that can affect the validity of a functional analysis?

A. The use of a single setting for the analysis

B. The use of multiple participants for the analysis

C. The use of a latency-based measurement system

D. The use of a restricted range of antecedent stimuli

84)   Over time, the IOA between two observers gets better because they have come to an unspoken understanding about how to score topographies of the behavior, which is different from the operational definition. This is known as:

A. Expectancy.

B. Observer drift.

C. Reactivity.

D. B and C.

85) If the target behavior is dangerous, baseline:

A. Should be conducted by staff members trained in restraint procedures.

B. Should be conducted by large staff members.

C. Can be conducted but should be brief.

D. May not be possible due to safety concerns.

86) Which of the following could be a DV (dependent variable) for a child in a classroom?

A. Aggression

B. Rate at which the teacher delivers reinforcement

C. Number of correct math problems completed in a minute

D. Time from onset to completion

87) Working collaboratively with another professional or paraprofessional means:

A. Graphing blood levels and psychotropic medications on the same graph to analyze blood levels and sharing this with the psychiatrist.

B. Conducting a preference assessment to identify potential reinforcers that staff will use in your program.

C. Graphing target behaviors and the current medications on the same graph to evaluate psychotropic medication's effect and share this with the psychiatrist.

D. (All of the above)

88) A behavior analyst is supervising a BCaBA who is conducting a functional assessment. What should the behavior analyst do to ensure the assessment is being conducted ethically?

A. Observe the BCaBA's sessions and provide feedback

B. Provide the BCaBA with written instructions and checklists

C. Check in with the BCaBA periodically but allow them to work independently

D. Have the BCaBA record the assessment sessions for review later

89) The alternating treatments design controls for:

A. Sequence effects.

B. Generalization effects.

C. Implementation issues.

D. Efficiency effects.

90) Every day a student screams loudly and at various volumes in the classroom, school playground, and on the school bus. It only happens when there are other students around, so you hypothesize that the function is attention. Multiple baseline should be used across:

A. Interventions.

B. Students.

C. Behaviors.

D. Settings.

91) Parents say that they slowly stop implementing the behavior plan the days after the BCBA supervision visit. What should the BCBA do first?

A. Inform them that you will contact the appropriate funding and/or protective services agencies, if necessary.

B. Simplify the program, visit more often and stay in touch with the parents between the supervision visits. Make sure the plan is implemented accordingly and praise them when they do.

C. Write a plan that is easier for the parents to implement, even if it is less effective.

D. Discontinue services because the child is not benefitting from your services.

92) A DRO, DRI, and overcorrection procedures are just as good and effective at decreasing the child's SIB. What procedure should the BCBA choose?

A. The DRI or overcorrection procedure because they will teach new behaviors.

B. The overcorrection procedure because the self-injury is severe.

C. The DRO or overcorrection procedure because they are easier to implement.

D. The DRO or DRI, because when possible, reinforcement should be used.

93) A kid bites his hands when he's at school and the hypothesized function is to escape from demands and tasks. As a replacement behavior, you teach him to moan when he wants a break. What procedure is this?

A. DRA or DRC.

B. DRA or DRI.

C. DRI or DRC.

D. (All of the above)

94) How does the alternating treatment design address the issue of multiple treatment interference? It does so by:

A. Continuing the baseline.

B. Making the conditions highly generalizable.

C. Making the conditions highly discriminable.

D. Conducting a component analysis.

Shhhh...

95)   You read the behavior plan of a student and you notice that for the first 4 days there is no intervention, then 5 days where a token system is implemented, followed by 8 days with no intervention, and again a token system for four days. What kind of plan is this?

A. A-B-A-B

B. B-A

C. B-A-B

D. A-B-A-C

96)   You want a graph that shows and summarize how the aggressive behavior changed in response to three different procedures. You can use a:

A. Bar graph.

B. Cumulative record.

C. Equal interval graph.

D. (All of the above)

97)   You want to increase a child's rate of writing. Use a:

A. DRL.

B. DRI.

C. DRH.

D. DRO.

98)   Intraverbal training should:

A. Be incorporated into mand and tact training.

B. Not start until the student has a large repertoire of echoics, tacts, and mands in their vocabulary.

C. Begin after acquiring 20-30 mands.

D. Start when the child is good at echoing, imitating, and matching to samples.

99)   What is the primary function of a stimulus control procedure in behavior analysis?

A. To establish a new behavior

B. To maintain an existing behavior

C. To transfer a behavior from one context to another

D. To increase the generalization of a behavior

100)   The changing criterion design is a suitable methodology for:

A. Very dangerous behaviors.

B. Promoting generalization.

C. Teaching new skills.

D. Shaping behavior rates.

101)   Which is the correct analysis?

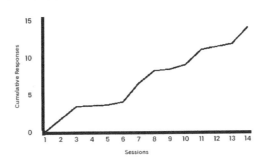

A. (Not a cumulative graph)

B. An initial high rate, followed by no responding, then a slowly increasing rate

C. A high rate at first, followed by no responding, then by a variable rate of responding.

D. No responding, followed by an increasing rate, then no responding

102)   When would it be ideal to try to increase the time between responses (interresponse time)?

A. A student often doesn't finish his math tests because after answering each math problem, he just sits there and stares the wall.

B. A student engages in self-stimulatory behavior during academic tasks because the therapist is delivering NCR (Noncontingent Reinforcement) too infrequently.

C. A student isn't doing well in school assignments because the therapist delivers noncontingent reinforcement too frequently.

D. (All of the above)

103)   Once the behavior is recorded, the person collecting the data doesn't have to watch for the rest of the interval. What procedure is it?

A. Continuous procedure.

B. Whole-interval procedure.

C. Event recording procedures.

D. Time sampling measurement procedure.

104) The student's behavior can be measured directly (by rate, duration, etc.) or indirectly by:

A. Reviewing attendance records.

B. Measuring permanent products of the behavior.

C. Interviewing teachers and staff.

D. Interviewing the child.

105) You are evaluating the efficacy of an intervention to help the members of a little league baseball team improve their throwing accuracy. The intervention, to be implemented over the course of the baseball season, takes place during brief training sessions at the beginning of every team practice. Your evaluation is at risk of a confound due to:

A. Bootleg reinforcement.

B. Client attrition.

C. Maturation.

D. Changes in the environment.

106) When implementing aversive techniques, Behavior Analysts should consistently:

A. Use a very high-performance standard for training, implementation, and monitoring the procedure with supervision.

B. Increase their own weekly hours with the client.

C. Use video to supervise implementation remotely.

D. Use only RBTS or staff who have worked in the field at least 3 years and have developed positive rapport with the client.

107) You want to decrease the aggression of one child in the classroom, and you think that peer pressure will work. Which group contingency would be the best fit?

A. Interdependent

B. Dependent

C. Good Behavior Game

D. Independent

108) When the teacher says, "Please sit," the student does just that. For the student, this is an example of:

A. Expressive language.

B. Manding.

C. Intraverbal language.

D. A listener skill.

109)   Paul's mother has started putting candy in his lunch, and he has stopped working for candy at school. This is an example of confound due to:

A. Maturation.

B. Changes in the environment.

C. Client attrition.

D. Bootleg reinforcement.

110)   After completing baseline and three sessions of the experimental phase, your client moves to another state. This exemplifies an experimental confound due to:

A. Client attrition.

B. Bootleg reinforcement.

C. Maturation.

D. Changes in the environment.

111)   A therapist-implemented intervention to improve reading resulted in no improvement on a standardized test; however, the teacher maintains that the intervention enhanced interest in reading.

A. This reflects a socially valid outcome.

B. This reflects internally and socially valid outcomes.

C. Determine social validity by conducting a functional analysis of reading.

D. This is an internally valid outcome, but not a socially valid one.

112)   What is the purpose of a cumulative record graph in behavior analysis?

A. To display trends in behavior over time

B. To compare data from multiple participants

C. To analyze the effectiveness of an intervention

D. (All of the above)

113)   You want to increase the frequency of a new behavior and then make it resistant to extinction. Which reinforcement schedules would be optimal?

A. FR 1, then VR 3, then VR 8

B. FR 2, then VR 3, then VR 8

C. VR 1, then VR 3, then VR 1

D. FR 8, then VR 3, then FR 1

114) The Behavior Analyst Certification Board:

A. Has the authority to suspend or revoke certification for Code violations.

B. If a BCBA/BCaBA is reported for an ethical violation, certification will be immediately revoked; reinstatement is possible following due process.

C. Has the same ethical code as most other professions.

D. Is primarily concerned with maintaining a good name for the field of ABA.

115) What best defines a socially valid procedure?

A. It produces a meaningful change in the life of the individual.

B. It is accepted by the individual and their community.

C. The interventions are effective and relevant to change the targeted behavior.

D. All of the above.

116) In the first condition, the average of SIB is about 35% of intervals. After the introduction of thr intervention, the average is about 15% of intervals. What could you say about the SIB in the graph as a result of the intervention that was implemented after Session 3?

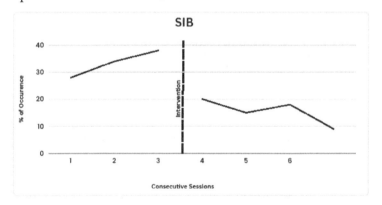

A. We can't say for sure that the intervention caused any changes.

B. The level after the onset of the intervention is stable.

C. We can assert that the intervention was effective in reducing SIB.

D. The intervention caused a 50% reduction in SIB.

117) Testimonials for use in published materials should come from:

A. Anyone.

B. Former clients.

C. Current and former clients.

D. Current clients.

118)   Hand-over-hand prompts were used by the therapist to help the child to put on a shirt. This is an example of:

A. Physical cue.

B. Position cue.

C. Stimulus prompt.

D. Response prompt.

119)   Aggression may emerge when utilizing reinforcement in a behavior change program:

A. When other people in a group share the same reinforcers due to limited availability.

B. When a target behavior does not occur, but the reinforcer is delivered anyway.

C. When a reinforcer is withheld because the target behavior was not emitted.

D. When individuals earn reinforcement for the entire group rather than for themselves alone.

120)   This is a _____ graph.

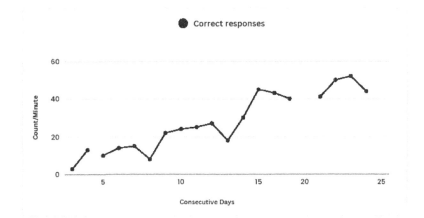

A. Cumulative record

B. Equal-interval

C. Bar

D. Semi-log

121)   A behavior analyst is supervising a trainee who is having difficulty with a client's behavior. The trainee is unsure of how to proceed and has asked the behavior analyst for advice. What should the behavior analyst do?

A. Tell the trainee what to do

B. Ask the trainee questions to help them problem-solve the situation

C. Ignore the trainee's request for advice

D. Reprimand the trainee that he does not know what to do

122) On the bowling shoes, the size is written on the back of each shoe. This is a good example of:

A. A stimulus prompt.

B. A verbal prompt.

C. An SD.

D. A model response prompt.

123) A child wouldn't do his work in class, so the teachers started to use escape extinction. The child behavior got worse and increased in intensity. You suggest that:

A. Teaching and reinforcing acceptable ways to request breaks.

B. Adding a verbal reprimand.

C. Adding a response cost.

D. Continuing the intervention as is for another week.

124) Which of the following is NOT a core ethical principle of behavior analysis?

A. Professional Competence

B. Integrity

C. Confidentiality

D. Objectivity

125) A scatter plot enables an analysis of behavior:

A. Across random events.

B. Across times of the day.

C. Under controlled conditions.

D. Given certain activities.

126) A solid line connects the data points in the first condition. Then other 6 data points are connected by a separate solid line in a second condition.
Which of the following best describes the graph?

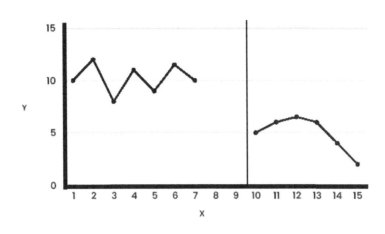

A. Low, variable responding followed by low, stable responding in the same phase

B. High, stable responding followed by a decreasing trend in the second phase

C. High, variable responding followed by low, stable responding in the same phase

D. Low, stable responding followed by low, stable responding in the same phase

127) Which of the following best describes a visual representation of a behavioral assessment that you should show the client? Information is shown:

A. In a way that the individual can comprehend.

B. In conformance with APA Guidelines.

C. In Excel or other widely used format.

D. So that other behavior analysts can easily interpret the data.

128) A gymnast has a baseline average of 50 pull-ups correctly completed in 10 minutes, with a high score of 60. Her coach set target performance at 75 correct pull-ups. Which would be an appropriate shaping criterion to reach that goal?

A. Reinforce only 58 or greater correct pull-ups; then advance to the highest score minus 2 with each new high score.

B. Reinforce only 40 or greater correct pull-ups; advance by 5 pull-ups when the criterion is reached twice.

C. Reinforce only 52 or greater correct pull-ups; advance by 10 pull-ups when the criterion is reached twice.

D. Reinforce only 52 or greater correct pull-ups; advance to the average correct plus 2 when the criterion is reached twice.

129) Maria is a 7-year-old girl with autism who engages in self-injurious behavior by hitting her head against the wall. After conducting an FA, the function of the behavior seems to be sensory, to access automatic reinforcers. Which of the following is the most appropriate behavior intervention plan for reducing Maria's self-injurious behavior?

A. Providing Maria with a helmet to wear to prevent head injury

B. Using a token economy to reward Maria for not engaging in self-injurious behavior

C. Teaching Maria alternative ways to engage in self-stimulation and reinforcing appropriate behaviors

D. Punishing Maria for engaging in self-injurious behavior

130) Your daughter wants to improve her dancing movements. You decide to use a shaping procedure. The first thing to do is:

A. Define her performance goal.

B. Model the desired behavior.

C. Determine the shaping steps.

D. Identify the reinforcer.

131) An 11th-grade high-functioning student who does well in school agrees that a BCBA assesses his ritualistic habits and creates a behavioral plan. The BCBA does not get permission from the minor's parents. Would this be appropriate?

A. No, consent should have been obtained because the behavior is potentially stigmatizing.

B. No, consent must be obtained from the parents because the child is a minor.

C. Yes, since the child is close to adulthood.

D. Yes, since the student is high functioning and the behavior occurs publicly.

132) In ABA, the goal of a single-subject graph is to:

A. Show the data to best persuade the viewer of the correct conclusions.

B. Show that a change in the dependent variable was followed by a major change in the independent variable.

C. Let the data show as clearly as possible how related the dependent and independent factors are.

D. Show that change in the IV (independent variable) was followed by a major change in the DV (dependent variable).

133) Which is an example of a comparative analysis?

A. None of these are a comparative analysis

B. A DRO FI 15 minute is compared to a DRO FI 10 minute procedure for hand mouthing.

C. A mand training program is compared to another mand training program.

D. A time-out plus token economy treatment for aggression is compared to baseline.

134)   At the supermarket, a toddler demands candy and throws a tantrum when told "No." When this occurs, the parent never gives him the candies, yet the tantrums continue. The tantrums could continue because:

A. The tantrum is receiving reinforcement of parent attention.

B. The parent does not combine extinction with a punishment procedure. x

C. It is a way for the child to get even with the parent.

D. The tantrum is an elicited emotional response.

135)   Jane is a Registered Sleep Therapist (RST) and a Board Certified Behavior Analyst (BCBA). In her flyer, next to the description of RPT should be:

A. A statement that RST is a novel intervention method that isn't yet supported by the literature.

B. A disclaimer stating that RST is not a behavior-analytic method and is therefore not covered by her BCBA certification.

C. An explanation of the similarities and differences between behavior analysis and play therapy.

D. The official RST logo.

136)   A BCBA has recently put some of his studies into a book for practitioners. If he talks about the outcomes of interventions that have already been published, he:

A. Must make his data publicly available.

B. Must include references to these publications.

C. Previously published data cannot be used.

D. May include the data without references to their prior publication.

137)   For a child who hits himself in the head with his hands, you can teach him to ride a scooter with both hands. What kind of process does this describe?

A. DRD

B. DRH

C. DRI

D. DRO

138)   For which skill are you most likely to use a chaining procedure?

A. Sitting with good posture

B. Fluffing a pillow

C. Making toast

D. Becoming a nurse

139) Which exemplifies a parametric analysis of protective equipment?

   A. Gloves applied by a teacher, teacher's assistant, and assistant principal

   B. A helmet applied contingent upon all identified precursor behaviors

   C. A helmet applied for 1, 2, 3, and 4 different behaviors

   D. Gloves with no fingers, 1/4 fingers, 3/4 fingers, and full fingers

140) Which function(s) do the data support?

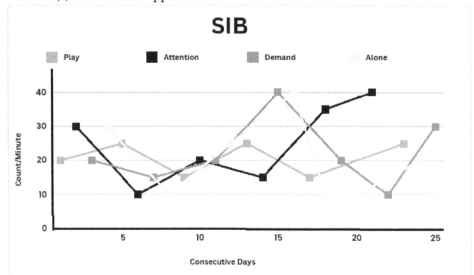

The ordinate (Y axis) is labeled 'Count per Minute' and the abscissa (X axis) is labeled 'Consecutive Days' and there are 25 total sessions. The data series data points are distinguished by different symbols and colors. There is one condition per session.

   A. Demand

   B. Tangible

   C. Attention

   D. Undeterminable

141) Once a month, a teenager with a severe intellectual disability gets aggressive "out of the blue," as reported by the staff. You should:

   A. Conduct a descriptive assessment.

   B. Conduct an FA (functional analysis).

   C. Conduct a functional analysis using interviews, scatterplot data, and ABC data instead of analog experimental conditions.

   D. Assume the behavior is maintained by automatic reinforcement and train staff on managing aggressive behavior.

142) What is the term for a procedure in which a target behavior is gradually modified by reinforcing successive approximations of the desired behavior?

A. Differential reinforcement

B. Extinction

C. Shaping

D. Punishment

143) A resident walks into the kitchen of the group home and screams and kicks the cabinets until a worker comes. The worker then gives a glass of water to the resident:

A. The screams and kicks are not a mand because no words are used.

B. The screams and kicks are under the control of an AO for water.

C. Functional Communication Training may be appropriate to teach the resident to pour himself a glass of water.

D. Functional Communication Training may be appropriate to teach the resident a more appropriate mand for water.

144) A child is throwing toys in the classroom. You recommend ignoring the behavior but the teacher is concerned about imitation by other children. You should recommend

A. Using a time-out procedure.

B. Using extinction for a day and monitoring the behavior.

C. Using a response cost procedure.

D. Using a differential reinforcement procedure.

145)   The ordinate (Y axis) is labeled 'Occurrences per Hour' and the abscissa (X axis) is labeled 'Consecutive Days.' Each condition is distinguished by different symbols and colors.
Which function do the data support?

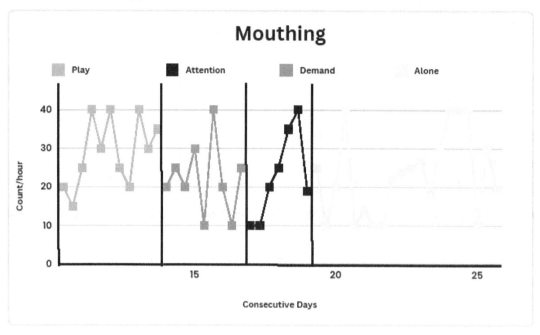

A. Demand, automatic reinforcement, attention, play

B. Automatic reinforcement or undeterminable

C. Automatic reinforcement, attention, demand

D. Attention and demand

146)   A child touches his teacher's hair because she always reprimands him for it. An extinction procedure would involve:

A. Discontinuing social and tangible reinforcement until the behavior stops.

B. Ignoring the behavior.

C. The teacher not being distracted and continuing the demands.

D. Redirecting this child to another activity.

147)   For a child who bangs his head against a table, a sensory extinction method would be?

A. To pad the table.

B. Reinforce incompatible behavior (e.g., talking to others) and provide a contingent reprimand.

C. Ignore the head banging.

D. Reinforce incompatible behavior (e.g., talking to others).

148)   A child engages in SIB in an austere environment. An NCR intervention is implemented which involves activity items. The intervention eliminates the SIB:

  A. The intervention was an extinction procedure.

  B. SIB will likely recur if the activity items are removed.

  C. The SIB behavior was extinguished.

  D. (All of the above)

149)   Which function(s) do the data support?

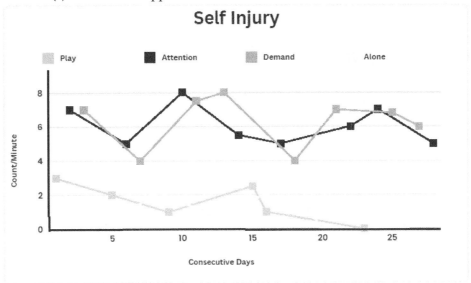

  A. Automatic reinforcement

  B. (Undeterminable)

  C. Attention and escape

  D. Escape and automatic reinforcement

150)   Which of the following is likely a motivating operation, and therefore, may occasion a mand?

  A. Providing a meal, but no utensils

  B. Providing a pencil and paper

  C. Providing a book

  D. (All of the above)

151)   What is the purpose of a behavioral assessment in behavior analysis?

  A. To diagnose a psychological disorder

  B. To identify environmental variables that influence behavior

  C. To evaluate the effectiveness of a behavioral intervention

  D. To prescribe medication for behavior problems

152) A teacher wants to increase the number of students who turn in their homework on time. The behavior analyst recommends providing immediate feedback and praise to students who turn in their homework on time. What type of consequence is being used in this scenario?

　A. Negative punishment

　B. Positive punishment

　C. Negative reinforcement

　D. Positive reinforcement

153) A behavior analyst is supervising a trainee who is implementing an intervention that is not part of the behavior plan. The trainee believes that the intervention will be effective and wants to try it. What should the behavior analyst do?

　A. Allow the trainee to implement the intervention

　B. Explain to the trainee why the intervention is not part of the behavior plan and instruct them to follow the plan

　C. Add the intervention to the behavior plan and document it

　D. Report the trainee to the BCBA for implementing a nonscientific intervention.

154) Which of those options is not a behavior analytic principle?

　A. Positive reinforcement

　B. Negative punishment

　C. Introspection

　D. Shaping

155) A client may receive treatment for an ear infection as you are about to begin an intervention. To be able to experimentally evaluate the intervention, you should:

　A. Extend your baseline and encourage the doctor to postpone treatment.

　B. Begin both medical and behavioral interventions immediately.

　C. Encourage the doctor to postpone treatment and begin the behavioral intervention.

　D. Encourage the doctor to begin treatment and extend your baseline.

156) After less restrictive attempts have failed, you develop an intervention that includes an aversive component. You should always:

　A. Determine if the aversive component will result in a negative emotional response.

　B. Begin by collecting baseline data.

　C. Obtain consent from the client.

　D. Determine whether the program will be properly implemented.

157) An ethical consideration when using a multiple baseline design to evaluate self-injurious behavior is the:

   A. Risk of injury during the treatment phase.

   B. Limited internal validity of the multiple baseline design.

   C. Extended baseline for self-injury.

   D. Risk of injury during the reversal phase.

158) How is the reinforcer's value identified in a progressive ratio schedule? It is based on:

   A. Change in rate in a single behavior relative to baseline.

   B. The relative rates of responding between two schedules of reinforcement.

   C. The rate of an individual's selection of items when presented in an array.

   D. How many responses an individual will emit to earn the reinforcer.

159) Which of those options is not a discriminative stimulus?

   A. A green traffic light

   B. A red stop sign

   C. The sound of a dog barking

   D. The taste of chocolate

160) A BCBA is working with a client who has a history of physical aggression. The client's parent requests that the BCBA use physical punishment to decrease the aggression. According to the ethical code, what should the BCBA do in this situation?

   A. Agree to the parent's request and use physical punishment as a behavior intervention

   B. Refuse the parent's request and explain why physical punishment is not an appropriate behavior intervention

   C. Use physical punishment as a behavior intervention but only if it is the client's preferred method of intervention

   D. Consult with other professionals before making a decision about using physical punishment as a behavior intervention

161) A behavior analyst is using an ABAB design to evaluate the effectiveness of an intervention. What is the purpose of the second "A" phase in the design?

   A. To replicate the baseline phase

   B. To evaluate the stability of the behavior change

   C. To confirm the effectiveness of the intervention

   D. (All of the above)

162) Which of the following is an example of a behavior cusp?

    A. Learning to brush one's teeth independently

    B. Learning to tie one's shoes

    C. Learning to ride a bike

    D. Learning to make coffee

163) Samantha is allergic to strawberries. One day, she ate a strawberry and had an allergic reaction, including hives and difficulty breathing. The next time she saw a strawberry, she became anxious and started to hyperventilate. Which type of conditioning is involved in Samantha's reaction to seeing a strawberry?

    A. Observational learning

    B. Respondent conditioning

    C. Operant conditioning

    D. None of the above

164) Incidental teaching:

    A. Is characterized by moment-to-moment decision-making with respect to the instructional method to use.

    B. Uses student-initiated behavior to prompt self-management strategies.

    C. Take advantage of natural situations and establishing operations (EOs) in the environment.

    D. Uses naturally occurring opportunities with no modifications to the environment.

165) Mark is a 10-year-old boy with ADHD who has difficulty completing homework assignments. Which of the following is the most appropriate behavior intervention plan for increasing Mark's completion of homework assignments?

    A. Using a token economy to reward Mark for completing homework assignments

    B. Punishing Mark for not completing homework assignments

    C. Providing Mark with extra time to complete homework assignments

    D. Teaching Mark self-monitoring strategies and reinforcing completion of homework assignments

166) A behavior analyst is working with a child who engages in aggressive behavior towards their peers. The BCBA conducts a functional analysis and determines that the behavior is maintained by access to attention from peers. What type of intervention is most appropriate in this scenario?

    A. Extinction

    B. Differential reinforcement of alternative behavior (DRA)

    C. Response blocking

    D. Punishment

167)   PSI is also known as:

A. Professional System of Instruction.

B. The Keller Plan.

C. The Skinner Plan.

D. Precision Teaching.

168)   You create a task analysis for "frying an egg" to be used with all residents of a large group home. You immediately start writing out the task analysis. It is likely that:

A. The task analysis is sufficient for all learners.

B. All the necessary steps have been included.

C. All the SDs for all of the component skills have been included.

D. It is too simple for some residents and too complex for others.

169)   Sarah is a 12-year-old girl with Down Syndrome who has difficulty following directions from her teacher. Which of the following is the most appropriate behavior intervention plan for increasing Sarah's compliance with teacher directions?

A. Punishing Sarah for not following directions

B. Providing Sarah with a preferred item or activity after following directions

C. Ignoring Sarah's noncompliant behavior and waiting for it to decrease on its own

D. Teaching Sarah to follow a visual schedule and reinforcing compliance with each step

170)   Alex is a 5-year-old boy with autism who engages in stereotypy (repetitive hand flapping) during circle time at school. Which of the following is the most appropriate behavior intervention plan for reducing Alex's stereotypy behavior?

A. Providing Alex with a preferred toy to play with during circle time

B. Ignoring Alex's stereotypy and waiting for it to decrease on its own

C. Teaching Alex a replacement behavior to engage in during circle time and reinforcing the replacement behavior

D. Using physical restraint to prevent Alex from engaging in stereotypy behavior

171)   With Precision Teaching, procedures are designed to promote?

A. Repetitive responding.

B. Fluency.

C. Precision.

D. (All of the above)

172) Choral responding (i.e., all students responding at the same time):

   A. Allows the teacher to monitor the performance of each student frequently.

   B. Group cohesion is promoted.

   C. Gives each student a chance to practice multiple times.

   D. (All of the above)

173) You might use a task analysis when teaching which behavior?

   A. Saying "I love you."

   B. Manding for grapes

   C. Waving goodbye

   D. Taking out the garbage

174) You are using a token system with higher-functioning individuals. To have the tokens acquire conditioned reinforcer qualities initially, you should:

   A. Have learners earn tokens by doing challenging, yet brief tasks, then have them exchange the tokens for reinforcers.

   B. Hand out tokens to learners to trade for reinforcers.

   C. Inform learners that they can trade their tokens for backup reinforcers with the earned tokens.

   D. Give learners tokens and reinforcers at the same time.

175) John is a 15-year-old boy with autism who engages in elopement (running away) behavior when he is in new or unfamiliar environments. Which of the following is the most appropriate behavior intervention plan for decreasing John's elopement behavior?

   A. Punishing John for eloping

   B. Providing John with a preferred item or activity to engage in when he elopes

   C. Teaching John to request a break or escape when he feels overwhelmed and reinforcing appropriate requests

   D. Using physical restraint to prevent John from eloping

176) A level system refers to a form of token economy that involves:

   A. Backup reinforcers are replaced with less valuable items and privileges as participants move up in the levels of the system.

   B. Reinforcement requirements are lowered at higher levels to support creative thinking and complex performances at higher levels.

   C. Participants progress from lower to higher degrees of reinforcement value based on their behavior meeting specific target criteria.

   D. (All of the above)

177) Your goal is to reduce your smoking cigarettes behavior. What could be a potentially effective component of self-management intervention if other aspects of self-management, such as data gathering and goal setting, are

already established?

    A. Your plan includes consequences determined by your friend or spouse.

    B. You read a book about will power and self-management.

    C. Your plan includes self-administered consequences.

    D. (All of the above)

178)   Amie is a 4-year-old girl who engages in aggressive behavior when she is denied access to a preferred toy. Which of the following is the most appropriate behavior intervention plan for reducing Jamie's aggressive behavior?

    A. Providing Jamie with the preferred toy as soon as she requests it

    B. Ignoring Jamie's aggressive behavior and waiting for her to calm down

    C. Teaching Jamie alternative ways to request the preferred toy and reinforcing appropriate requests

    D. Using physical restraint to prevent Jamie from engaging in aggressive behavior

179)   A client who is learning how to wash his hands has turned on the water on his own 3 times. The next step will be to wet his hands independently. This is an example of:

    A. Backward chaining.

    B. Concurrent chaining.

    C. Total task presentation.

    D. Forward chaining.

180)   What is an example of an implementation of the Premack principle?

    A. Provide a choice whether to complete the homework before or after the watching of a video.

    B. Complete homework, then go outside to play.

    C. Engage in outdoor activities for a duration of 15 minutes, followed by the completion of academic assignments.

    D. Play a video game, then do homework.

181)   Bill, a young individual in his adolescent years, has expressed experiencing feelings of anxiety when confronted with situations involving gatherings of individuals and social environments. The individual exhibits a preference for being alone since it serves as a means of mitigating feelings of anxiety. According to Bill's therapist, implementing strategies such as exposing Bill to social settings and engaging in activities that target his social skills could potentially alleviate his anxiety. The ability to make such assumption is mostly related to which philosophical perspective?

A. Mentalism

B. Methodological behaviorism

C. Structuralism

D. Radical behaviorism

182)   What statement is accurate?

A. The individual's phylogenic history influences both operant and respondent behavior.

B. Operant behavior is part of an individual's genetic endowment.

C. Respondent behavior, involuntary behavior that is elicited by unconditioned stimuli without prior learning, is mainly the result of the organism's phylogenic history.

D. The term 'phylogenic' describes behaviors learned over an individual's lifespan.

183)   The BACB Compliance Code indicates that you should _____ before starting a new client intervention:

A. Obtain extensive training on use of the intervention, including shadowing the first colleague, for at least one month to see it in practice.

B. Ensure that the seminal research on this topic was published in JABA.

C. Consult the literature to verify the intervention has been published within the last 10 years.

D. Assess whether the intervention employs procedures that have been scientifically validated.

184)   You have had extensive experience in using ABA with people who have autism, and your district has asked you to work with a young adult who has been given the diagnosis of emotionally disturbed that is deemed to be "out of control." You have limited training or expertise working with this group.

A. You cannot provide services because you lack this expertise.

B. You should consult an expert on the subject and look for their supervision.

C. You should provide services because you were asked by your employer.

D. You can conduct indirect assessments, but you cannot conduct experimental assessments or write an intervention.

185)   A client's potty-trained brother begins bedwetting. The parents requested the Behavior Analyst to suggest an intervention for bedwetting. What would you recommend to the parents?

A. Not provide any advice since he is there to provide services to the sibling.

B. Begin timed waking and trips to the bathroom every 2 hours.

C. Rule out medical causes before seeking behavioral treatment.

D. Try simply limiting liquids after 7 pm.

Shhh...

COFFEE AND NOTES

....

....

....

....

....

....

....

....

....

....

....

....

....

....

....

....

....

....

ANSWERS AND EXPLANATIONS

1)   B: Report the other behavior analyst's ethical violations to the appropriate authorities. Behavior analysts have an ethical obligation to report ethical violations by other behavior analysts to the appropriate authorities. This helps to protect clients and maintain the integrity of the field of behavior analysis.

2)   A: With a large group of talkers, it is difficult and time-consuming to identify individual loud or quiet talkers. Therefore, a contingency which provides a reward contingent upon the collective behavior of everyone is most practical. Moreover, peers are likely to be a positive influence.

3)   C: In reinforcer assessments, concurrent schedules of reinforcement are used to evaluate the relative reinforcing value of two stimuli. This is achieved by establishing contingencies between the stimuli and two distinct behaviors, and thereafter analyzing the individual's response across the available options.

4)   B: Refuse the parent's request and explain why the use of a non-scientifically validated communication device is not an appropriate behavior intervention. Behavior analysts should only use behavior interventions that are supported by research and that have been demonstrated to be effective. If a communication device has not been scientifically validated, it may not be an appropriate intervention for the client.

5)   A: A device used in operant conditioning experiments. The Skinner box, also known as the operant conditioning chamber, is a device used in operant conditioning experiments to study the behavior of animals, such as rats and pigeons.

6)   B: The results suggest that the attention condition may have functioned as a maintaining variable for the child's SIB, as the behavior occurred for the longest duration during this condition. It is not possible to draw conclusions about establishing or abolishing operations from these data alone.

7)   C: According to Skinner, it is illogical to believe that behavior acts on different principles only because it takes place inside an organism's skin. This statement arises from the requirement of empirical scientific methodology to come into direct contact with its subject matter, thus restricting the analysis of behavior to events that can be empirically observed.

8)   B: Requesting is the behavior; receiving the toy car is the reinforcer; the presence of the father is the discriminative stimulus. The reinforcer is provided by another person, so it can't be considered automatic but instead is socially mediated.

9)   D: ABA focuses exclusively on behavioral concerns that matter to the person involved or his community, employs diverse assessment techniques, and is rooted in the principles of behaviorism.

10)   B: Line graphs are commonly used to display data over time, making them an appropriate choice for displaying changes in behavior across baseline and intervention sessions.

11)   D: According to the Code, it's imperative to demonstrate competence and constantly review your knowledge following the latest scientific research. When addressing specific areas like pica disorders, in-depth knowledge and competence are paramount. Collaborative discussions with other professionals and an exhaustive review of relevant studies are necessary. Additionally, guidance, training and oversight from a behavior analyst expert in pica-related topics are essential.

12)   D: A reflex is a stimulus-response relationship in which an unconditioned stimulus elicits an unconditioned response reliably without any prior learning history.

13)   B: The EAB (Experimental Analysis of Behavior) is a scientific method where experiments to discover principles are conducted under controlled conditions, primarily in laboratory settings. Once identified, these principles become tools for applied practices targeting societal problems.

14)   C: When we discuss S-S relations, we're referring to Stimulus-stimulus relations such as conditional stimulus control. This highlights how stimuli within a class have equal effects on behavior.

15)   D: A respectable scientist consistently challenges scientific statements, always open to reconsidering long-accepted beliefs in light of new data. This aligns with the principle of philosophic doubt. Philosophical skepticism advises accepting these fresh insights until they're contested by further evidence. Recognize the value of this data as it introduces an alternate new perspective.

16)   D: In situations where someone holds significant power and authority, such as in teaching, or supervising roles, there's a potential for exploitation of students or research participants.

17)   D: In a functional analysis, the play condition is the one that eliminates the motivating operations prevalent in the other conditions. Attention and tangible items are easily accessible or offered on a dense reinforcement schedule, and the individual is not required to perform any tasks.

18)   B: Avoid reinforcers with potentially detrimental or unhealthy long-term effects. Additionally, whenever possible, avoid introducing something that must be eliminated later.

19)   C: Any challenging behavior, and particularly those that are novel or potentially harmful, should undergo a functional assessment. If the same behavior shows up in a new setting, another functional assessment is necessary.

20)   C: The aversive stimulus is added (i.e., father's reprimand) and follows the behavior (i.e., screaming) and decreases it over time. Therefore, it is positive punishment.

21)   A: A deterministic mindset identifies the events that precede and cause the behavior. A deterministic statement does not have to pinpoint a cause; it needs only to recognize the existence of a cause. Unpredictable tantrums are simply a description of the behavior. "We haven't yet identified the factors that control the tantrums," alludes to the fact that the behavior is caused by something.

22)   D: During the escape condition in a functional analysis, tasks and demands are placed.

23)   D: The smell of food causes salivation. A touch of something hot leads to a withdrawal reflex, and the cold wind will elicit goosebumps. These are examples of unconditioned responses to unconditioned stimuli.

24)   B: A group of stimuli that share a similar effect on a given response class is referred to as a stimulus class. For example, a whistle at a sports game and a raised red flag; can signal a foul and prompt the same reaction from the players. Stimuli that reinforce a specific behavior or those with shared physical traits can also bring about the same verbal response, making them part of a stimulus class.

25)   C: a paired-stimulus assessment. In a paired-stimulus assessment, two stimuli are presented together and the individual's preference for each is measured by comparing the duration of engagement with each stimulus.

26)   C: The ethical principles for RBTs and BCBAs specify that they should not start romantic relationships with clients, their parents, or supervisees for at least two years after the conclusion of their professional relationship.

27)   A: James was trained to understand that 'Cane' corresponds to 'Dog,' and 'Dog' signifies 'Perro.' However, the conclusion that 'Cane' stands for 'Perro' was not a part of his training, which makes it a derived relation. Reflexivity involves the learner selecting an identical stimulus. Symmetry comes into play when the learner, initially trained to choose B when given A, also learns to choose A when given B. Transitivity occurs when the learner, taught to select B from A and C from B, can also select A from C and C from A as a result of their training.

28)   B: Every instance of response gets reinforced each time, which is the principle of Continuous Reinforcement (CRF) or also termed Fixed Ratio 1 (FR1).

29)   D: With each call, a selling response is evoked. The event of making a sale (considered as reinforcement) may come about after an inconsistent number of responses (phone calls). This is characteristic of a Variable Ratio (VR) schedule.

30)   C: It is preferable to put all information into a formal written contract.

31)   C: Fixed ratio and variable interval. A mixed schedule of reinforcement involves 2 or more different schedules that alternate. In this scenario, Jenny is using a fixed ratio schedule (every 10 pages read) and a variable interval schedule (5 minutes of break time).

32)   D: A behavioral assessment is designed to identify the specific behavior to be modified and all relevant factors that could be useful for the intervention. Such aspects include resource availability, beneficial assets, caregivers or important people for the individual, competing contingencies, factors that can help maintain and generalize the behavior, and any potential reinforcers and/or punishers.

33)   B: Spontaneous recovery is the reappearance of a behavior during extinction despite the absence of reinforcement. This effect is temporary and is subsequently followed by a decrease in behavior.

34)   A: Using an experimental design and repeatedly observing a change in behavior due to the teacher's presence, a functional relationship is established, i.e., the variables of which the behavior is a function are identified.

35)   C: The protection of minors is our first priority. Behavior analysts pursue informal resolutions whenever possible. It is essential to observe that the scenario outlined in the question is neither an instance of abuse nor even a suspicion of abuse.

36)   C: The matching law efficiently delineates the corresponding rates of reinforcement delivered on different interval-based schedules. When a ratio schedule of reinforcement is in effect, behavior tends to adhere to the more dense schedule.

37)   D: Behavioral momentum is established by requesting high-probability behaviors via rapid, successive demands, potentially increasing compliance to a low-probability request. This intervention is known as a High-p request sequence.

38)   C: If it is necessary to prevent someone from getting harmed, you may be legally required to disclose information even without the client's permission.

39)   B: Supervisors only assign responsibilities and assignments that the supervisee can competently, ethically, and safely perform.

40)   D: The highly controlled experimental conditions of functional analysis may differ from those of the natural environment. When this is the case, various strategies are put into effect to enhance the ecological validity of the experimental setting, i.e., the degree to which conditions in the experimental setting correspond to those that influence behavior in the natural setting.

41)   A: Finny's new behavior of swimming to the top has been learned after multiple practices, and it constitutes operant conditioning. In fact, his behavior has been reinforced by a reward, the treat, until it became consistent, and it eventually started to occur even when the reinforcement was not present.

42)   B: Behavioral contrast is a phenomenon where changes to the reinforcement schedule of a particular behavior in one context can affect its frequency in a different context. For example, when a college professor like John institutes a rule limiting smartphone use in class, his students may start passing notes more frequently, demonstrating this principle of behavioral contrast.

43)   A: The differential response given the separate stimulus conditions implies that the behavior is under discriminative control. In other words, the basketball player has learned to discern the coach's specific hand claps. The term response maintenance describes the ongoing occurrence of the behavior even when the intervention has ended.

44)   C: Because of the very strong appetitive properties of the candy, he stares at it, tries to steal it, etc., rather than focusing on the instructional stimuli. Utilizing a less effective reinforcer or implementing a token system, such as poker chips, avoids the issue of reinforcers inciting or provoking behavior that is incompatible with the desired behavior.

45)   B: Stimulus generalization and setting/situation generalization are considered interchangeable words. Both phenomena pertain to the manifestation of conduct in the presence of stimuli that differ from those utilized during training. A modification in the environment results in a modification in the stimulus. Response generalization refers to the phenomenon where a new response that is functionally identical to the trained response is exhibited.

46)   D: While many behaviors may serve a specific function, it is often not possible to tell the function just based on the physical characteristics or appearance of the behavior. Self-injury may potentially fulfill various purposes, such as escaping from nonpreferred tasks, or to get access to a stuffed animal.

47)   C: Response generalization, commonly known as induction, involves generating versions of a learned behavior that are physically different yet functionally similar. This process results in a change in the behavior's form, but not its function. An example is a girl who learns to play a tune on the piano with her right hand and then independently learns to play it with her left hand.

48)   C: Lisa's statement is considered a mand. Her friend, as the listener, gives an intraverbal response.

49)   B: Discuss the discrepancy and work together to improve their agreement. IOA is an important quality control measure in behavior analysis. When there is a discrepancy between observers, the behavior analysts should discuss the discrepancy and work together to improve their agreement. This may include clarifying the definitions of the target behavior or providing additional training to one or both observers.

50)   A: At the beginning of the tact transfer procedure, multiple stimuli are introduced to induce the tact, along with multiple consequences. Once extraneous antecedent and consequent stimuli have been faded, the concluding step sees the nonverbal stimulus (the item) stimulating the tact, with generalized conditioned reinforcement like praise being the sole consequence.

51)   A: If an MO is not in effect (with or without an SD), a mand will not occur. The child's growling stomach indicates that some time has passed since he has eaten and food items are currently valuable as reinforcers. Upon seeing the cookie jar in the parent's presence, a mand for food occurs in the form of a request for a cookie.

52)   D: You've learned to smoothly alter the gears in a manual vehicle as a result of the driving instruction. Each successful transition between gears reinforces the gear-changing activity. This is now contingency-shaped behavior.

53)   C: Rule-governed behavior is essentially a verbal rule given to the individual that follows it. A rule is when you do not engage in a certain behavior not because you have come into contact with the contingencies before, but because of a rule you have been told about what could happen if you do engage in that behavior.

54)   D: The process for identifying a function is equivalent to identifying the reinforcer that maintains the behavior. A function refers to the antecedent event that serves as the motivating factor for an individual to engage in a certain behavior. For example, escaping nonpreferred tasks or demands, getting attention, and seeing the teacher getting frustrated and angry. While functions often involve public events that are observable stimulus changes evident by anyone, there are instances where the function is a private event, only subjectively experienced by the individual, and not observable. These private events can include the release of endorphins and sensory stimulation.

55)   D: End the personal relationship with the parent and refer the client to another behavior analyst. This question assesses your knowledge of the ethical code for behavior analysts. The ethical code prohibits behavior analysts from engaging in multiple relationships that could impair their objectivity or effectiveness in providing services to clients. If a behavior analyst has a personal relationship with a client's parent, it is their responsibility to end the personal relationship and refer the client to another behavior analyst.

56)   B: The absence of a fork when giving a plate of food enhances the value of a fork as a reinforcer. This is considered a CMO-T.

57)   A: The sign is a stimulus in the presence of which the response of taking the next exit has been reinforced by obtaining gas and in the absence of which taking the next exit has not been reinforced. That is, the sign exerts discriminative control over taking the next exit--an SD. (The gas gauge on empty would be the CMO-T).
The sign is a stimulus in the presence of which the response of taking the next exit has been reinforced by obtaining gas and in the absence of which taking the next exit has not been reinforced. That is, the sign exerts discriminative control over taking the next exit--an SD. The CMO-T would be the gas gauge on empty.

58)   D: The blurry words may have an abative effect (decrease current reading), an evocative effect on looking for glasses (increase looking for glasses), and/or an abative effect on reading (decrease reading).

59)   D: The therapist who enters the room has the role of a CMO-R due to the fact that the occurrence of a tantrum leads to a delay in the start of the session.

60)   C: Consider a store scenario. A position cue is when a specific product is strategically placed to be the closest or most easily accessible to the shopper, subtly suggesting its selection. Movement cues can be associated to an employee gesturing towards or adjusting a product to draw attention. Physical prompts might be equated to an associate handing a product to the shopper. On the other hand, redundancy prompts are techniques like enlarging a product image, spotlighting it, or adding distinctive markers to make it stand out.

61)   C: Functional communication training (FCT). In this scenario, the behavior analyst has determined that the SIB is maintained by escape from academic demands. The most appropriate intervention in this case is to teach the child a more appropriate way to escape academic demands, such as through functional communication training (FCT).

62)   B: Individual supervision. In this scenario, the behavior analyst is experiencing difficulty understanding how to complete an assessment. Individual supervision would be most appropriate, as it would allow the supervisor to provide focused, one-on-one guidance and support.

63)   D: "Functional analysis" is typically used to refer to experimental demonstrations. Indirect methodologies involve getting information without direct observation of the behavior in question. Interviews and rating scales are considered to be indirect methods.

64)   B: Emily's reaction to hearing a car horn is based on respondent conditioning, where the antecedent stimulus (the car horn) elicits an involuntary response (anxiety and fear) due to the pairing with the unconditioned stimulus (the car accident and injury).

65)	A: Experiencing sharp pain from touching a hot stove serves as a UMO, which tends to evoke immediate behaviors to relieve the pain. Concurrently, this sensation can abate one from touching hot surfaces again in the future, due to its punitive aftereffect (these effects counteract each other).

66)	B: "Trials to criterion" refers to the number of response opportunities required for an individual to meet a predetermined performance criteria.
"Frequency," also referred to as count, is defined as the total number of responses recorded within a fixed time interval.
"Duration" refers to the temporal span from the initiation and termination of a given response.
"Celeration" refers to the quantification of change by comparing two response rates and dividing it by the corresponding time interval between the two response rates.

67)	C: The terminology "novel setting" or "in the presence of stimuli" could be technical for certain non-expert audiences. Straightforward terminology that is readily comprehensible to the recipient should be used, while ensuring that your simplified explanations remain correct and accurate.

68)	B: Address the issue with the trainee and discuss the importance of punctuality. Behavior analysts have an ethical responsibility to provide effective supervision. This includes addressing performance issues with the trainee. The behavior analyst should discuss the importance of punctuality with the trainee and work with them to find a solution to the problem.

69)	C: Episodes of crying often have no clear beginning and end, and may vary widely in duration.

70)	C: "Celeration" refers to the quantification of change by comparing two response rates and dividing it by the corresponding time interval between the two response rates.
"Frequency," also referred to as count, is defined as the total number of responses recorded within a fixed time interval.
"Duration" refers to the temporal span from the initiation and termination of a given response.
"Rate" refers to the number of responses within a certain unit of time, such as seconds, minutes, or hours.
"Trials to criterion" refers to the number of response opportunities required for an individual to meet a predetermined performance criteria.

71)	C: If a different person completes the exam, it is not reflective of an individual's own performance. This means that the test lacks validity.
"Validity" is achieved when a measure accurately assesses the construct it intends to evaluate.
"Accuracy" refers to the degree to which a measurement accurately represents or nearly approximates the actual true value.
"Reliability" refers to the consistency of obtaining the same outcome while measuring the same event multiple times.
"Interobserver agreement" refers to the degree two observers agree on the results of their assessments.

72)	B: The explanation of assessment outcomes is communicated using accessible language and visually presented in a format that both the client and their representative may comprehend. In the event that the client is unable to comprehend the results, the explanation provided to the surrogate will be sufficient.

73)   D: Fixed ratio schedule. Here, the behavior analyst applies a fixed ratio of reinforcement, where a reward is given after a predetermined number of responses. In this context, the reward is the reduced price when buying multiple product units.

74)   B: Indirect assessments are considered, for example, interviews, surveys, and checklists. Direct assessments are considered the observations of the client within their natural environment or the permanent products derived from the behaviors of the individual that are then examined. A functional analysis involves changing the IV while observing the changes in the DV during direct observations.

75)   A: To establish a new behavior. In this scenario, the primary function of PECS is to establish a new behavior, specifically the ability to request items using pictures. This can increase the child's communication skills and decrease frustration and problem behavior.

76)   B: "Validity" refers to the measure's ability to correctly evaluate the intended attribute.
"Accuracy" refers to how closely a measurement mirrors the real or true value.
"Reliability" involves the consistent reproduction of the same result when measuring an event repeatedly.
"Interobserver agreement" measures the extent of agreement between two observers during their observations.

77)   B: The phenomenon of "reactivity" refers to the alteration of an individual's behavior due to the mere presence of an observer.
"Observer drift" refers to the phenomenon when observers gradually alter their operational definitions over a period of time.
"Complexity" refers to the presence of complex data gathering systems, such as those involving many target behaviors or participants, which are susceptible to unreliable data collection.
The concept of "expectancy" refers to the presence of bias resulting from preconceived assumptions and the provided information.

78)   B: Consult with other professionals to determine the appropriate next steps. This question assesses your knowledge of the ethical code for behavior analysts. The ethical code requires behavior analysts to seek consultation and collaboration with other professionals when they are unsure of how to proceed with a client's behavior intervention plan. Continuing with an ineffective behavior intervention plan or modifying the plan without consultation can be harmful to the client and may violate the ethical code.

79)   A: BCBA must deliver feedback in a manner that is advantageous to the supervisee. Code violations should be promptly resolved, involving all parties in the matter. In the event that a resolution cannot be achieved, the supervisee should initiate the process of filing a formal complaint to the Behavior Analyst Certification Board (BACB).

80)   C: Reliability refers to the degree of consistency in observed data and the phenomena being measured. Accuracy refers to the degree to which a measurement accurately represents or nearly approximates the underlying value.

81)   C: Accuracy refers to the degree to which a measurement accurately represents or nearly approximates the actual value.

Reliability refers to the consistency of obtaining identical outcomes while measuring the same phenomenon multiple times.

Interobserver agreement refers to the degree of consensus between two observers collecting data for the same phenomena.

Validity refers to the extent to which a data collection system accurately measures the intended construct or phenomenon.

Believability refers to the degree to which individuals are convinced by the accuracy of certain measures.

82)   D: The exclusion of previously failed treatments cannot be entirely ruled out, however, it is generally advisable to refrain from their utilization. Treatment outcomes are more likely to be successful for interventions that have demonstrated effectiveness in the past.

83)   A: The use of a single setting for the analysis. The validity of a functional analysis can be affected by a number of factors, including the use of a single setting for the analysis. This can limit the generalizability of the results and make it difficult to determine whether the observed behavior is specific to the setting or is a more general characteristic of the individual's behavior.

84)   B: "Observer drift" refers to the phenomenon wherein observers gradually alter their operational definitions over a period of time.

The phenomenon of "reactivity" refers to the alteration of behavior due to the mere presence of an observer.

"Complexity" in data collection systems, such as those involving several target behaviors or participants, can lead to issues of data collection reliability.

The concept of "expectancy" refers to the presence of bias resulting from preconceived assumptions and the facts provided.

85)   D: The primary goal of a baseline condition is to provide a reference point for evaluating and comparing the effects of a treatment intervention. For this reason, the baseline takes place prior to the intervention but it should be avoided in those situations where it poses a risk to safety (for example, when collecting data for severe behaviors like SIB, aggression, elopement, etc.)

In this particular scenario, baseline should not be collected and treatment may start right away.

86)   C: The independent variable (IV) refers to the intervention that the practitioner implements to see changes in the target behavior. For example, introducing a medication, starting a token reinforcing system, using prompts to increase likelihood of correct responding, implementing NCR procedure, etc. The dependent variable (DV) refers to the behavior of interest and how it is measured and quantified. For example, rate of SIB, duration of sitting and attending, and latency of responding to questions. The DV is considered both the target behavior and its measurement.

87)   C: Collaboration means working with other experts in order to accomplish a desired clinical outcome. Collaborating does not mean assuming the responsibilities of that professional.

88)   A: Observe the BCaBA's sessions and provide feedback. In this scenario, the behavior analyst is responsible for ensuring that the functional assessment is being conducted ethically. The most effective way to do this is to observe the BCaBA's sessions and provide feedback in real-time.

89)   A: The alternating treatments design effectively controls some threats to validity thanks to its quick variation of conditions. Threats to validy include: maturation, data instability, sequence effects, and attrition. Maturation refers to the changes that take place in the subject throughout the course of the experiment. Data instability pertains to the variability that may hide the effects due to overlapping data points. Sequence effects arise when a condition that is run for multiple sessions influences the subsequent condition. Lastly, attrition refers to the loss of subjects during the study.
Implementing the same treatment for many sessions in a study has the potential to impact the subsequent condition, as observed in a withdrawal/reversal design. The utilization of rapid alternation serves to limit the occurrence of the sequence effect.

90)   D: It is not feasible to demonstrate the impact across several behaviors as the focus is solely on a single targeted behavior. While the issue manifests itself in diverse contexts, it is probable that a shared underlying function exists, given the same behavior observed across all situations. The intervention could be implemented in a sequential manner, using a multiple baseline design across different settings.

91)   B: In the event that the implementation of the behavior analytic program is impeded by environmental factors, the behavior analyst endeavors to mitigate the impact of these limitations by either removing them entirely or documenting the barriers preventing their removal. Several strategies for enhancing the program's implementation may be considered, such as simplifying the program without compromising its efficacy, increasing the frequency of visits, and reinforcing parental adherence to the program. These techniques are implemented to alleviate environmental limitations.

92)   D: Whenever feasible, it is advisable to prioritize the utilization of reinforcement procedures over punishment methods, especially when both approaches are considered equally successful.

93)   A: Differential Reinforcement of Alternative behavior (DRA) is when appropriate and desirable behaviors are reinforced while the target behavior is placed on extinction. Differential Reinforcement of Incompatible behavior (DRI) is a particular example of DRA where the appropriate behavior is incompatible with, or cannot be performed simultaneously with, the problem behavior. The alternative behaviors need to have the same function as the problematic behavior. DRC refers to reinforcing communicative behavior such as "May I have a cookie," which serves as an alternative to stealing cookies. Note that the behaviors of moaning and hand-biting can coexist and are not incompatible.

94)   C: The quick alternation of conditions may make it difficult for behavior to come under stimulus control of the contingencies operating in the different conditions and can cause confusion. Distinctive signals can be employed to help distinguish between these conditions. As an example, a coach might blow a specific whistle tone for one condition and a different tone for another. A clear antecedent signal integrated into the intervention, like different colored flags in a team game, can help discriminate the conditions.

95)   A: The letter "A" is the baseline condition, whereas the letter "B" is one intervention condition, and the letter "C" is a second intervention condition.

96)   A: "Bar graphs" are commonly utilized to present summary data.
"Line graphs" are commonly employed to represent the continuous measurement of behavior over a period of time.
"Pie graphs" are commonly utilized to visually represent the proportion of a whole or to break it into distinct portions.
The "cumulative record" is a graphical representation in the form of a line graph that displays the cumulative occurrences of a particular behavior across time.
"Equal interval graphs" are a type of line graph that have axes with equal interval scales.

97)   C: With DRH (Differential Reinforcement of a HIGH rate), reinforcement is contingent upon the behavior meeting or exceeding a particular rate (e.g., writing 20 words per minute).

98)   B: The initiation of intraverbal training should be postponed until a kid has developed proficient skills in echoic, imitations, mand, tact, and matching-to-sample.

99)   A: A stimulus control procedure is a technique that manipulates and changes antecedent stimuli to teach the desired new behavior. By arranging specific antecedent stimuli in the setting, the BCBA enhances the probability that the targeted behavior will occur in the presence of those stimuli.

100)   D: The criteria that is changed refers to a specific measurement, typically the rate, of a target behavior. In the changing criterion design behaviors are already in the client's repertoire. We are just increasing or decreasing a dimension of that known behavior. This design is not for learning new behaviors, it does not serve to generalize behaviors and it is not appropriate for behaviors for which there is very little tolerance.

101)   C: A flat line indicates a lack of response. A steep line indicates a high rate of response. A line exhibiting a variation in slope signifies a variable rate in responding.

102)   C: The interresponse time refers to the time between consecutive responses. If the frequency of a response is excessively high (happening too much), it is appropriate to set the goal to increase the interresponse time.

103)   D: Time sampling measurement procedures involve recording whether a behavior happens or doesn't happen within a set interval or noting if it took place at its conclusion. Continuous measurement, on the other hand, demands the consistent logging of every single instance of a particular behavior. When using event recording methods, continuous observation is essential to ensure that every instance of the behavior is noted.

104)   B: The method of measuring through permanent products involves measuring the alterations in the environment that result from the behavior itself. Permanent items can be categorized into two types: natural permanent products, such as a spelling or math test, and contrived permanent products, such as a photograph or a video of the natural permanent products.
Interviews are a form of indirect assessment that yields qualitative data in the form of anecdotal data. This does not qualify as a measure of behavior.

105)   C: "Maturation": refers to changes that take place in a subject during an experiment that are unrelated to the independent variable.
"Client attrition": refers to the loss of experimental subjects before the experiment is finished.
Changes in the environment": refers to uncontrolled changes that could affect the dependent variable.
"Bootleg reinforcement": refers to a participant gaining access to reinforcement independent of the experimental contingencies.

106)   A: BCBAs will enhance training, monitoring, and oversight supervision to ensure treatment fidelity when implementing aversive or punishing procedures.

107)   B: To modify an individual's behavior, a dependent group contingency can effectively use peer influence with a specific focus on the behavior of the targeted person.

108)   D: "Listener training" is synonymous with "Receptive language training." Listener skills, also known as receptive language, consist of correctly responding to verbal instructions.

109)   D: "Bootleg reinforcement": refers to a participant gaining access to reinforcement independent of the experimental contingencies.
"Client attrition": refers to the loss of experimental subjects before the experiment is finished.
"Maturation": refers to changes that take place in a subject during an experiment that are unrelated to the independent variable.
"Changes in the environment": refers to uncontrolled changes that could affect the dependent variable.

110)   A: "Client attrition": refers to the loss of experimental subjects before the experiment is finished.
"Maturation": refers to changes that take place in a subject during an experiment that are unrelated to the independent variable.
"Changes in the environment": refers to uncontrolled changes that could affect the dependent variable.
"Bootleg reinforcement": refers to a participant gaining access to reinforcement independent of the experimental contingencies.

111)   A: The lack of effect on standardized tests indicates that there is not an internally valid outcome; however, the teacher's assertion indicates a socially valid outcome.

112)   A: To display trends in behavior over time. A cumulative record graph is a type of graph used in behavior analysis to display the cumulative number of responses emitted over time. This type of graph can be useful in analyzing the trend of behavior and identifying changes in behavior over time. Trend and level is not shown in the graph to analyze the effect of the intervention and it can't be use to compare data from multiple people.

113)   A: Reinforce the behavior every single time at the beginning of the intervention, then space out the rewards and use a less dense and variable schedule of reinforcement.

114)   A: Behavior analysts must know the ethical Code. The certification may be revoked by the BACB in cases where ethics violations have been committed. In order to fulfill this objective, it is mandatory for Board Certified Behavior Analysts (BCBAs) to complete a total of four hours of ethics training throughout each certification cycle.

115)   C: Social validity is determined by how meaningful the target behaviors are to the individual, the acceptability of the intervention methods by the individual and the community, and the relevance and importance of the changes seen in the target behavior.

116)   A: Given that an AB design was used in this study, the variations in the data between the two phases do not provide sufficient evidence to establish a causal relationship. The data in each phase can be described; however, it is not possible to make definitive claims that the intervention caused the effects observed.

117)   B: Individuals who have not personally received your services would not be a trustworthy source of information. It is recommended that testimonials intended for publishing be only sourced from individuals who have previously been in a professional relationship with your and received your service.

118)   D: Response prompts don't change the task itself but are direct cues for the correct response. These hints can be spoken clues (verbal prompts), physical help (partial or physical prompts), or showing by example (modeling). The prompts help the client find the right answer. In the other hand, stimulus prompts operate directly on the antecedent to lead to the right answer alongside the critical SD.

119)   C: The manifestation of aggression in relation to the utilization of reinforcement arises as a consequence of extinction, specifically when the individual is unable to obtain the reinforcer. Having a limited resourse of reinforcers could also evoke violence, but solely in situations where there is a sense of competition to win the reinforcers. Programs that promote collaboration among individuals and peers are associated with a reduced likelihood of exhibiting aggressive behavior.

120)   B: This is an equal-interval graph with an overall increasing trend and low variability. At first glance, it could be confused with a cumulative graph, in which the daily number of responses is added to the sum of all previous numbers; but on days 8 and 14, the data point is below the previous data.

121)   B: Ask the trainee questions to help them problem-solve the situation. Supervision is an opportunity for the trainee to learn and develop their skills. The behavior analyst should use this opportunity to help the trainee problem-solve the situation, rather than simply telling them what to do. By asking questions and guiding the trainee, the behavior analyst can help the trainee develop their own problem-solving skills.

122)   C: Prompts are temporary stimuli. The numbers on the shoes are a permanent feature. This is simply an SD.

123)   A: The exclusive implementation of escape extinction raises ethical considerations. It is imperative to allow students to have breaks when they ask appropriately. Teaching the student a functional alternative behavior can effectively decrease the occurrence of an extinction burst and emotional responses.

124)   D: The four core ethical principles of behavior analysis are Professional Competence, Integrity, Confidentiality, and Responsibility.

125)   B: A scatter plot is a graphic display used to discover the temporal distribution of target behavior. It visually displays the relationship between variables such as time of day, session, period, etc. along one axis, and the day or date along the other axis. It shows whether the behavior's occurrence is typically associated with certain time periods.

126)   B: In the first phase, the data are at a high level and stable (small ups and downs). After the phase line, the data indicate a downward trend.

127)   A: The assessment outcomes are explained using appropriate terminology and visually shown through visual graphs, ensuring comprehension for both the client and their representative. In the event that the client is unable to comprehend the results of the assessment, the explanation provided to the surrogate will be sufficient.

128)   D: It is desirable for the criterion to systematically increase in steps. Rapid progression may pose challenges that exceed one's capabilities, resulting in a decline in performance. If one progresses at a slow pace, there is a possibility that performance will reach a plateau.

129)   C: This question assesses your ability to design a behavior intervention plan based on the function of behavior. Self-injurious behavior is maintained by automatic reinforcement, meaning that the behavior itself is reinforcing. The most appropriate behavior intervention plan would be to teach Maria alternative ways to engage in self-stimulation and reinforce appropriate behaviors.

130)   A: The first step is to determine precisely the performance goal.

131)   B: In the case of a minor client, obtaining parental or surrogate consent is a necessary need for all behavior interventions and procedures.

132)   C: Single-subject graphs show the progression of an individual's behavior over time. They also demonstrate the degree to which the IV (intervention) changed the DV (behavior). An ABA design should not aim to convince the practitioner of any conclusion as the data presented on the graph should solely display the relationship between the variables.

133)   C: Comparative analysis involves comparing two or more independent variables (interventions) in a multielement design. A criticism to this type of analysis is that it focuses on "what is the best intervention" instead of understanding the behavior itself.
A comparative analysis can be conducted to examine the differences between two competing interventions, for example, a novel intervention with an existing one, a standard intervention with a refined one, or an intervention under different contextual circumstances.

134)   A: When you stop rewarding a behavior (extinction), it can lead to emotional or aggressive reactions. These reactions can be hard to overlook. Even if you're not giving the candy, paying attention to the behavior can still be reinforcing. For the process to work and extinction to be effective, attention to these emotional or aggressive behaviors should be minimal or close to zero.

135)   B: When engaging in professional activities or promoting oneself as a behavior analyst, it is advisable to only rely on one's behavior analytic qualifications and credentials. In the context of promoting non-behavior-analytic methods, it is imperative to provide a disclaimer explicitly indicating that the BCBA credential does not cover such interventions.

136)   B: The utilization of preexisting data must explicitly specify its prior publication status, along with appropriate referencing.

137) C: DRI is the reinforcement of a particular behavior that is incompatible with the target behavior. Toy play and head hitting cannot occur at the same time.

138) C: Chaining procedures, such as forward and backward chaining, as well as total task chaining, are used in the context of multi-step skill training. These techniques are particularly useful when the skill is not yet present in the individual's existing repertoire. A behavior chain is created using a task analysis that breaks down a complex behavior into small, teachable steps of the chain.

139) D: This does not represent a range of values.

140) D: Note that the rate of self-injury is undifferentiated among conditions, which indicates an automatic reinforcement function or that a function could not be determined.

141) A: Due to the severe and sporadic nature of the behavior, it would be inadvisable to proceed with a functional analysis (FA). Functional analysis (FA) procedures often involve conducting experimental sessions to determine the function of the behavior and when it is likely to occur. In this case, if conducting an FA, the number of responses obtained would likely be insufficient for a comprehensive analysis of the conditions, unnecessarily increasing the risks.

142) C: Shaping involves reinforcing successive approximations of the target behavior, gradually molding the behavior into the desired form.

143) D: Functional Communication Training (FCT) teaches better ways to communicate instead of engaging in problem behaviors. The procedure is first to find out why the maladaptive behavior is happening (the function) and then teach an alternative behavior to get the same reward.

144) D: Extinction is not recommended in situations where the replication of severe behavior from peers is a matter of concern. In order to effectively address the inappropriate behavior, it is necessary to implement a procedure that not only eliminates the target behavior but also reinforces a desired and more appropriate behavior.

145) B: An undifferentiated pattern suggests an automatic reinforcement function or the function cannot be determined.

146) B: The reinforcer is the negative attention. Therefore, extinction would involve not providing that attention.

147) A: With sensory extinction, you mask or prevent the sensory stimulation-in this case, pad the table.

148) B: Giving other things to focus on might decrease self-harming, but it won't eliminate it. If you take those activities away, the harmful behavior might return. This is not an extinction procedure.

149) C: Note that the rate of self-injury is consistently highest in the attention and demand conditions.

150) A: If a book is provided to a child, he can start reading it. He can write if you give him a paper and a pencil. Given the child a plate of food with no utensils, the fork increased its value as a reinforcer.

151)   B: To identify environmental variables that influence behavior. The purpose of a behavioral assessment in behavior analysis is to identify the environmental variables that influence behavior, including antecedent stimuli and consequences. This information is used to design effective interventions that can increase desired behaviors and decrease problematic behaviors.

152)   D: Positive reinforcement. In this scenario, the consequence of providing immediate feedback and praise is being used as positive reinforcement to increase the behavior of turning in homework on time.

153)   B: Explain to the trainee why the intervention is not part of the behavior plan and instruct them to follow the plan. Behavior analysts should only implement interventions that are supported by research and have been demonstrated to be effective. If an intervention is not part of the behavior plan, the behavior analyst should explain to the trainee why it is not appropriate and instruct them to follow the plan.

154)   C: Introspection is not a behavior analytic principle. Behavior analysis is a science that focuses on observable and measurable behavior, rather than subjective experiences.

155)   D: Possible medical causes of behavior problems should be addressed prior to or at the same time that the problem is being addressed with a behavioral intervention. Of course, if you want to experimentally evaluate the behavioral intervention, you cannot implement behavioral and medical interventions simultaneously.

156)   D: A well-written program is useless if it is not going to be carried out properly. Sometimes you will get consent from a parent/guardian (not the client) and begin with an intervention (not baseline).

157)   C: An ethical consideration of the withdrawal design is the risk of injury during the reversal phase and for the multiple baseline design, it is an extended baseline.

158)   D: In a progressive ratio schedule of reinforcement, the student is asked to systematically increase the number of responses to obtain the reinforcer. This analysis is valuable in assessing the effectiveness of a given reinforcer when there is an increase in response effort or a thinner schedule of reinforcement.

159)   D: A discriminative stimulus (SD) is an antecedent stimulus that evokes a specific behavior due to a history of reinforcement in the presence of that antecedent stimulus. The signal tells you that reinforcement is available. The taste of chocolate does not function as an SD as it does not signal the availability of reinforcement for any behavior.

160)   B: Refuse the parent's request and explain why physical punishment is not an appropriate behavior intervention
This question assesses your knowledge of the ethical code for behavior analysts. The ethical code prohibits the use of physical punishment as a behavior intervention. It is the BCBA's responsibility to educate the client's parent about the risks and negative effects of using physical punishment and to provide alternative evidence-based behavior interventions.

161)   B: To evaluate the stability of the behavior change. In an ABAB design, the second "A" phase is used to evaluate the stability of the behavior change that was observed during the first "B" phase. This phase can help determine whether the behavior change was a result of the intervention or whether it was due to other factors, such as natural fluctuations in behavior. If the behavior change remains stable during the second "A" phase, this provides additional evidence that the intervention was effective.

162)   C: Learning to ride a bike. A behavior cusp is a behavior change that has far-reaching effects on an individual's life, opening up new opportunities and experiences. Learning to ride a bike is an example of a behavior cusp because it can lead to increased independence, social interaction, and physical activity.

163)   B: Respondent conditioning. Samantha's reaction to seeing a strawberry is based on respondent conditioning, where the antecedent stimulus (seeing a strawberry) elicits an involuntary response (anxiety and hyperventilation) due to the pairing with the unconditioned stimulus (allergic reaction).

164)   C: The primary application of incidental teaching is in the training of communication skills. Naturally occurring establishing operations (EOs) are utilized as circumstances to strategically change the environment, creating favorable conditions for the learner to engage in mands (requests) and tacts. In this scenario, the student is presented with an assignment that lacks materials, creating a situation for the student to request for it. Therefore, the instructor has created an EO.

165)   D: Teaching Mark self-monitoring strategies and reinforcing completion of homework assignments. This question assesses your knowledge of behavior change strategies. The most effective behavior intervention plan for increasing homework completion would involve teaching Mark self-monitoring strategies and reinforcing completion of homework assignments, rather than punishment or simply providing more time. A token economy may also be effective if properly implemented, but self-monitoring should be the first step.

166)   B: Differential reinforcement of alternative behavior (DRA). In this scenario, the behavior analyst has determined that the aggressive behavior is maintained by access to attention from peers. The most appropriate intervention in this case is to teach the child an alternative, appropriate way to gain attention from peers, such as through differential reinforcement of alternative behavior (DRA).

167)   B: The Personalized System of Instruction (PSI), often known as the Keller Plan, was established by Fred Keller during the 1960s. Originally, it was developed as an instructional approach for higher education settings, but it has subsequently been implemented across diverse disciplines and educational levels.

168)   D: You can create a task analysis by doing the task yourself, get guidance from an expert or watching someone else competent, but it must be individualized to the client. When developing a task analysis, it is important to take into account the learner's abilities and prior experience. A task analysis designed to be universally applicable may prove to be overly simplistic for certain learners and excessively intricate for others. This is NOT a "one-fits-all" approach.

169)   D: Teaching Sarah to follow a visual schedule and reinforcing compliance with each step. This question assesses your knowledge of behavior change strategies. The most effective behavior intervention plan for increasing compliance with directions would involve teaching Sarah to follow a visual schedule and reinforcing compliance with each step. Punishment is not an effective strategy for increasing compliance, and ignoring noncompliance may reinforce the behavior.

170)   C: Teaching Alex a replacement behavior to engage in during circle time and reinforcing the replacement behavior. This question assesses your ability to design a behavior intervention plan based on the function of behavior. Stereotypy is often maintained by automatic reinforcement, meaning that the behavior itself is reinforcing. The most appropriate behavior intervention plan would be to teach Alex a replacement behavior to engage in during circle time and reinforce the replacement behavior.

171)   B: Precision Teaching methods are specifically developed with the objective of facilitating fluent responding, which entails the ability to provide accurate responses without any hesitation. The behavior exhibited by the learner suggests a high level of proficiency in the curriculum, as demonstrated by a reduction in the time taken to respond and an increase in the frequency of responses.

172)   D: In contrast to the conventional lecture structure that involves sporadic questioning of individuals, choral answering enhances group cohesion. This method allows educators to regularly assess the academic progress of individual students and offers them multiple opportunities to practice the correct responses.

173)   D: Task analyses are used to teach multi-step skills, such as tasks consisting of multiple steps or difficult skills that need to be brake down into simple components.

174)   C: To mitigate potential issues, it is advisable to refrain from placing any demands on the client at first. For those with higher cognitive abilities, it is advisable to provide a clear and concise explanation regarding the option to acquire reinforcers through earned tokens.

175)   C: Teaching John to request a break or escape when he feels overwhelmed and reinforcing appropriate requests. This question assesses your ability to design a behavior intervention plan based on the function of behavior. Elopement behavior is often maintained by escape from aversive or overwhelming situations, which is an example of negative reinforcement. The most appropriate behavior intervention plan would be to teach John to request a break or escape when he feels overwhelmed and reinforce appropriate requests. Punishment and physical restraint should be avoided as they may increase the likelihood of elopement behavior.

176)   C: In a level system, individuals progress or regress within a levels contingent upon their performance. Higher degrees of achievement are associated with more privileges, incentives, and require adherence to higher standards of performance. The token reinforcement schedule is also thinned to promote greater independence and maintenance of the behavior by matching the reinforcement schedules found in natural environments.

177)   B: Self-management needs the individual to be responsible for identifying and, in the majority of instances, implementing their own consequences and gathering their own data. The concept of willpower does not align with the principles of behavioral strategies.

178)   C: Teaching Jamie alternative ways to request the preferred toy and reinforcing appropriate requests. This question assesses your ability to design a behavior intervention plan based on the function of behavior. Aggressive behavior is maintained by access to preferred items or activities, which is an example of positive reinforcement. The most appropriate behavior intervention plan would be to teach Jamie alternative ways to request the preferred toy and reinforce appropriate requests.

179)   D: "Forward chaining" is a sequential process that involves teaching the step in the chain and subsequently incorporating each subsequent behavior one by one.

In "backward chaining" we initially teach the final step of the sequence, followed by the addition of the second-to-last step.

"Total task chaining," often referred to as concurrent chaining, is teaching each step in a sequential manner during each instructional session.

180) B: The Premack principle says that in order to engage in a high probability behavior (playing outside), compliance to a low probability behavior is required (doing homework). It is the "First, Then" procedure, also called Grandma's Law.

181)   D: This is a radical behaviorism perspective because environmental factors (i.e., social settings and social skills) are suggested to be the possible causal factors of anxiety.

182)   C: Learning derived from the interaction between the organism and its environment is called "Ontogenic," while behavior that's a product of genetic inheritance is termed "Phylogenic." Typically, operant behavior derives from ontogenic history and respondent behavior from phylogenic history. A behavior is 'evoked/emitted' if it's learned through consequences (operant) while it is 'elicited' for respondent behaviors.

183)   D: BCBAs base intervention decisions on scientifically and clinically derived knowledge. This may include articles from behavior analytic journals, assistance from colleagues, data gathered during treatment, and other academic materials based on sound scientific principles.

184)   B: Behavior analysts ensure they operate within the boundaries of their training and competence. If a request from an employer steps outside of these ethical confines, the BCBA has the choice to either lean on the expertise of an experienced professional in the field or delegate the task to another professional with more competence in the area.

185)   C: Prior to implementing a behavior analytic intervention, a reasonable medical consultation should be conducted to rule out contributing factors of a behavior. After the medical consultation, if the parents decide to pursue behavioral treatment, the BCBA must modify the professional relationship accordingly.

COFFEE AND NOTES

Answers Sheet

1. ___	27. ___	53. ___	79. ___
2. ___	28. ___	54. ___	80. ___
3. ___	29. ___	55. ___	81. ___
4. ___	30. ___	56. ___	82. ___
5. ___	31. ___	57. ___	83. ___
6. ___	32. ___	58. ___	84. ___
7. ___	33. ___	59. ___	85. ___
8. ___	34. ___	60. ___	86. ___
9. ___	35. ___	61. ___	87. ___
10. ___	36. ___	62. ___	88. ___
11. ___	37. ___	63. ___	89. ___
12. ___	38. ___	64. ___	90. ___
13. ___	39. ___	65. ___	91. ___
14. ___	40. ___	66. ___	92. ___
15. ___	41. ___	67. ___	93. ___
16. ___	42. ___	68. ___	94. ___
17. ___	43. ___	69. ___	95. ___
18. ___	44. ___	70. ___	96. ___
19. ___	45. ___	71. ___	97. ___
20. ___	46. ___	72. ___	98. ___
21. ___	47. ___	73. ___	99. ___
22. ___	48. ___	74. ___	100. ___
23. ___	49. ___	75. ___	101. ___
24. ___	50. ___	76. ___	102. ___
25. ___	51. ___	77. ___	103. ___
26. ___	52. ___	78. ___	104. ___

105. ___	133. ___	161. ___
106. ___	134. ___	162. ___
107. ___	135. ___	163. ___
108. ___	136. ___	164. ___
109. ___	137. ___	165. ___
110. ___	138. ___	166. ___
111. ___	139. ___	167. ___
112. ___	140. ___	168. ___
113. ___	141. ___	169. ___
114. ___	142. ___	170. ___
115. ___	143. ___	171. ___
116. ___	144. ___	172. ___
117. ___	145. ___	173. ___
118. ___	146. ___	174. ___
119. ___	147. ___	175. ___
120. ___	148. ___	176. ___
121. ___	149. ___	177. ___
122. ___	150. ___	178. ___
123. ___	151. ___	179. ___
124. ___	152. ___	180. ___
125. ___	153. ___	181. ___
126. ___	154. ___	182. ___
127. ___	155. ___	183. ___
128. ___	156. ___	184. ___
129. ___	157. ___	185. ___
130. ___	158. ___	
131. ___	159. ___	
132. ___	160. ___	